SCOTLAND'S SPORTING BUILDINGS

The practice of sport is a human right.
Every individual must have the possibility of
practicing sport, without discrimination of any kind
and in the Olympic spirit, which requires mutual
understanding with a spirit of friendship,
solidarity and fair play.
THE OLYMPIC CHARTER

TAM
ARTE
QUAM
MARTE

Scotland's Sporting Buildings

NICK HAYNES

HISTORIC SCOTLAND
Edinburgh 2014

Published by Historic Scotland
Longmore House · Salisbury Place
Edinburgh EH9 1SH

Text © Historic Scotland and the author

Nick Haynes asserts the moral rights to be identified
as the author of this work

Unless stated otherwise, all the illustrations in this
book are © Nick Haynes

ISBN 978 1 84917 150 2

All rights reserved. No part of this publication may be
reproduced, stored in a retrieval system, or transmitted,
in any form, or by any means, without the permission of
the publisher

Front cover: Aberfeldy Bowling and Tennis Pavilion

Back cover: Thomson's Tower, Duddingston

Frontispiece: Troon Golf Club (detail of façade)

Designed and typeset in Sweet Sans by Dalrymple
Printed on Condat Matt 150gsm and bound by
Butler Tanner & Dennis, Frome

www.historic-scotland.gov.uk

If you have enjoyed this book, you may like *Scotland's
First World War* and *Scotland's Canals*, which will be
available in autumn 2014. Both titles are published by
Historic Scotland.

For Ben, Millie and Lexi

The author would particularly like to thank Elly
McCrone (HS), Janis Adams, Professor Grant Jarvie
(Chair of Sport at the University of Edinburgh) and
Ranald MacInnes (HS) for their support, enthusiasm
and expertise.
  A great many other people have contributed
to the research and production of this book, for
which the author is extremely grateful: Michelle
Andersson (HS); Zach Anthony; Chris Asensio; Una
Bartley; Simon Blackett; Iain Brodie; Ross Brown;
Graham Callander (Royal Burgess Golfing Society
of Edinburgh); Kitty Chilcott; Heather Coady; Linda
Coxhead; Devon DeCelles (HS); Ian Elder-Cheyne;
Lydia Fisher (RCAHMS); Andrew Fleming; Lesley
Ferguson (RCAHMS); Philip Graham (RCAHMS);
Neil Gregory (RCAHMS); Roger Griffith (Eglinton
Country Park); Fiona Jamieson; Daniel Killeen; Chloe
Kippen; Euan Leitch; Jennie Marshall; Debbie Mays
(Royal Incorporation of Architects in Scotland);
Dawn McDowell (HS); William Meston (Braemar
Royal Highland Charity); Graham Mill (Cardross Golf
Club); Sarah Montgomery; Simon Montgomery (HS);
Ashley Moon (Hamilton Park Racecourse); Shona
Munro; Victoria Murray (HS); Craig Nisbet (Braemar
Gathering Annual); Steven Orr; Tom Parnell; Dr
Alison Rosie (National Records of Scotland); Clare
Sorensen (RCAHMS); Vanessa Stephen; James Turner
(HS); Ruth Whatling; Andrew Wilson; Maggie Wilson
(National Museums Scotland); and Michael Yabsley
(Eglinton Country Park). NH

HISTORIC SCOTLAND
ALBA AOSMHOR

Portobello Bathing Pool, poster by Tom Curr, about 1936
Photo: RCAHMS

The Portobello Bathing Pool, designed in Art Deco style by Ian Warner of the City Engineer's Department in 1934–6, was built to Olympic specifications with the added attractions of underwater floodlights and an electric wave-making machine. The pavilion contained a restaurant, ballroom and observation balcony. The 'most up-to-date swimming pool in the world' opened on 30 May 1936 with spectacular displays of 'high and fancy diving' in front of the 10,000-strong crowd. The opening ceremony also featured the Police Pipe Band and the Women's League of Health and Beauty, who, clad in silk blouses and sateen shorts, 'went through difficult movements with perfect grace and unison in pouring rain'. The complex was demolished in 1989.

Preface

In the year that Scotland plays host to the Commonwealth Games for the third time, this book is compiled to celebrate the diverse range and outstanding quality of historic purpose-built sporting architecture that exists across the country. Building upon the nationwide review of sporting buildings by Historic Scotland, the book is intended to be a selective introduction, rather than a comprehensive catalogue, drawing on Scotland's listed sporting buildings, which are important not only to the country's built heritage, but also for their significance in the recreational, social, economic and educational life of local communities.

The buildings included in the book extend beyond the officially recognised sports and para-sports of the Commonwealth Games to some of Scotland's most ancient and popular sports, such as golf, curling and horse-racing. The number of historic buildings linked with some sports is high, so only a representative selection can be illustrated here, while other sports have few or no associated historic listed buildings. Some sports never had much in the way of permanent accommodation, while changing times and fashions have all but eradicated the built heritage of other once-popular sports, such as quoiting. This book focuses on public sporting buildings and older sports with codified rules, which enabled them to be played on equal terms in more than one location. Most of the illustrated buildings are to be found in Lowland Scotland. Although various kinds of sport have always flourished in the Highlands and Islands, many of the buildings associated with these tend to be on private sporting estates, which are largely outwith the remit of this book.

ARRANGEMENT

The book is arranged by sport. Each chapter sets out a brief history of a sport, or group of sports, followed by a more detailed study of selected examples of associated architecture. In order to keep the book to a manageable size on such a broad subject, it has been necessary to largely exclude a number of sporting facilities: sporting spaces and landscapes (without buildings or structures); field, gun and motor sport buildings; buildings associated with dancing, yachting, canoeing, rambling, orienteering, mountaineering and skiing; private sporting estates; educational facilities (schools, colleges and universities); military facilities; and buildings under thirty years old. The sports histories at the beginning of each section are intended to outline the development of the oldest, or principal, sport that contributed to the building type, not every sport that is, or has been, associated with the illustrated buildings. In many cases, sporting venues now host a number of sports, for example, historic swimming pools now accommodate swimming and a range of associated sports such as diving, synchronised swimming, synchronised diving, water polo, triathlon and pentathlon. Early athletics and track cycling facilities developed out of sports days held in cricket and football grounds, so are not described separately.

BUILDING TYPES

Scotland's historic sporting buildings fall into four broad categories: specialist buildings for housing a sport (e.g. swimming pools); buildings for housing equipment and associated facilities (e.g. curling huts); buildings for socialising (e.g. golf clubhouses); and buildings for spectators (e.g. football stands). Often there is overlap between the categories, where buildings accommodate the sport, equipment, social spaces and spectators (e.g. ice rinks).

ACCESS

Many of the buildings featured in this book are open to the public at advertised times for normal sporting participation or events, but others are private. Inclusion of a building in this publication does not indicate any right of public access.

HS: Historic Scotland
RCAHMS: Royal Commission on the Ancient & Historical Monuments of Scotland

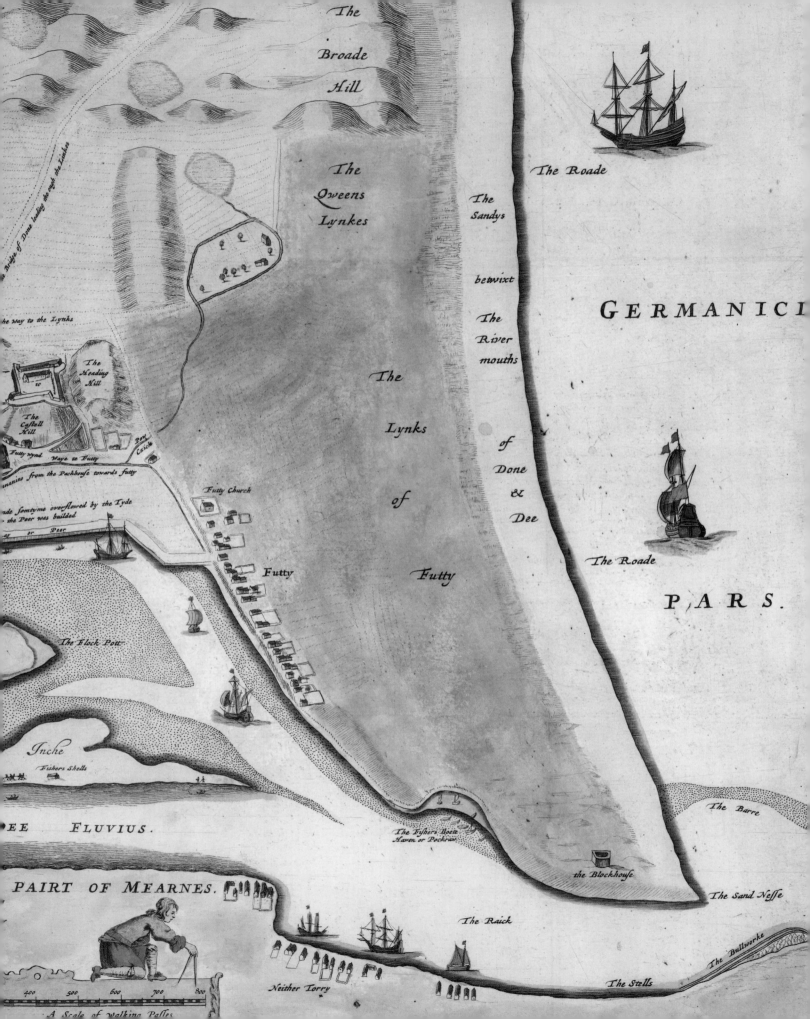

Scotland's Sporting History

MEDIEVAL AND RENAISSANCE

And amongst all vnnecessarie things that are lawfull and expedient, I thinke exercises of the bodie most commendable to be vsed by a young Prince, in such honest games or pastimes, as may further abilitie and maintaine health.

King James VI and I, *Basilikon Doron*, 1603

Several sports represented in this book have been practised in Scotland in one form or another for many centuries. Some, such as archery, Highland games and horse-racing, developed from the practise of military skills or competition at tournaments. Others, including football, golf, shinty, curling, bowling and tennis, grew out of both elite and less structured forms of popular sport. Evidence for the precise nature of sports practised by the labouring classes in the medieval and renaissance periods is difficult to establish, as rules were unwritten and probably varied from place to place. Several Acts of Parliament and Town Council Acts of the fifteenth and sixteenth centuries banned football, golf and shinty, probably the rough early forms of the games played in kirkyards and other urban spaces, which often resulted in damage to buildings, injuries to participants and passers-by, and occasionally even deaths. Increasingly during this period, sporting activities were encouraged to

Plan of Aberdeen by James Gordon of Rothiemay, 1661
National Library of Scotland, Edinburgh (detail)

'Vpon the east syd of the citie and of Futtie ther lyes many fair feilds, fruitfull of corns, quheat, bear, oats, pease, and pot hearbs and roots. Thes are marched by the feilds near the sea syde called the Lynks. The most remarkable amongst thes is the fair plaine called the Queens Links, the reassone of the name unknown. The Lynks extend themselves almost betuixt the two rivers of Done and Dee. I leer the inhabitants recreat themselves with severall kynds of exercises, such as foot ball, gotfe, bowlling, and archerie. Heer lykewayes they walk for ther health, Nixt to thes is the sea shore, plaine and sandie, wher at low water ther is bounds for horse races no less then two mylls of lenthe. (James Gordon of Rothiemay, *Abredoniae Utriusque Descriptio*, 1661)

occupy 'burgh commons' on the edge of the towns by means of charters.[1] One such was that granted by Bishop Hamilton of St Andrews in 1552 allocating the town's western links for 'golfe, futeball, shuting and all games'. Further north, records of golf on the links at Dornoch date from 1616. All burgh commons were crossed by rights of way and used for many other purposes, such as grazing, drying fishing nets, garment bleaching, mineral extraction, milking cows, markets, troop reviews and other events, which often came into conflict with the sporting activities. In spite of this, the common lands and adjacent beaches of Scotland's burghs became the playgrounds for the towns' inhabitants, accommodating sports such as horse-racing, golf, curling, kyles ('Dutch pins' or skittles), bowling and archery. The seasons dictated when some sports were played: the long summer grass for grazing made golf impossible, so autumn to spring months were favoured; curling obviously depended on freezing winter temperatures. The reformed church of the late sixteenth century made frequent interventions to try to prohibit Sunday sports, or at least to ensure that sports did not deter attendance at the kirk.

Until the middle of the eighteenth century wealthy individuals were responsible for the construction of most sport-related buildings in Scotland, as there were no sporting clubs or societies before that period. There is significant evidence in accounts and other documents for several sports as royal and courtly activities, particularly from the reign of James IV (1488–1513) onwards.[2] An enclosed space for war-like tournaments *à outrance*, called a 'barras' or 'barrace', had existed below Edinburgh Castle since the reign of Robert I (1306–1329), but under James V (1513–1542) 'lists', or semi-permanent spectator stands, were built of timber at Holyroodhouse and Stirling Castle for more chivalrous tournaments *à plaisance* (jousting).[3] Also constructed for James V is the earliest surviving sporting building in Scotland, the royal tennis court at Falkland of 1539–41, which is documented in the accounts of the Lord High Treasurer of Scotland.[4] James V's daughter, Mary,

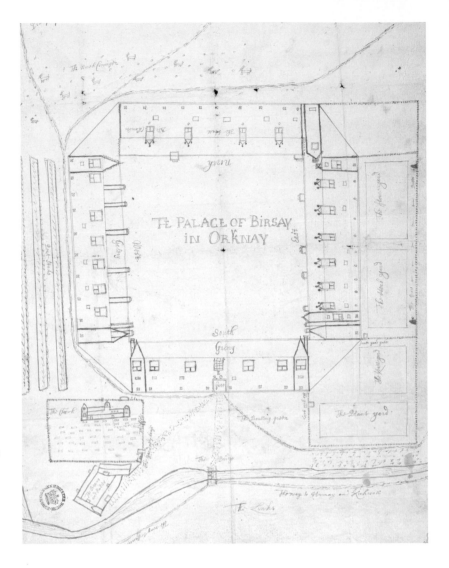

Plan of the Earl's Palace, Birsay, Orkney,
late seventeenth century
National Records of Scotland, Edinburgh

Robert Stewart, the illegitimate son of James V, built
the Earl's Palace at Birsay between 1569 and 1574.
The tyrannical Patrick Stewart extended and remodelled his father's palace from 1593 until his execution
in 1615. The abandoned palace was much decayed by
the time of this drawing. However, the plan is interesting for its identification of the sporting facilities
surviving from this once great residence. A 'Boulling
green' is marked beside the main south entrance, and
'The Bow Butts' are shown along the inside of the
eastern wall of the garden.

Queen of Scots, was by reputation a keen sports-
woman, practising riding, hunting, archery, tennis
and golf, and watching football during her captivity
at Carlisle Castle. In 1599 Mary's son, James Vi
and I (1566–1625) wrote a treatise on government, *Basilikon Doron* [royal gift], in the form of a
private letter to his eldest son and accomplished
sportsman, Henry, Duke of Rothesay. A revised
edition, published in London following James's
accession to the English throne in 1603, expands on
the importance of certain types of sport as virtuous
and kingly activities:

And amongst all vnnecessarie things that are lawfull
and expedient, I thinke exercises of the bodie most
commendable to be vsed by a young Prince, in such
honest games or pastimes, as may further abilitie
and maintaine health. For albeit I grant it to be most
requisite for a King to exercise his engine, which
surely with idlenesse will rouste and become blunt;
yet certainly bodily exercises and games are very
commendable; as well for bannishing of idlenesse
(the mother of all vice) as for making his body able
and durable for trauell, which is very necessarie
for a King. But from this count I debarre all rough
and violent exercises, as the foot-ball; meeter for
laming, then making able the vsers thereof: as
likewise such tumbling trickes as only serue for
Comedians and Balladines, to win their breade
with. But the exercises that I would haue you to
vse (although but moderately, not making a craft
of them) are running, leaping, wrastling, fencing,
dauncing, and playing at the caitche or tennise,
archery, palle maillè, and such like other faire and
pleasant field-games. And the honourablest and
most commendable games that yee can vse, are
on horsebacke: for it becommeth a Prince best of
any man, to be a faire and good horse-man. Vse
therefore to ride and danton great and courageous
horses; that I may say of you, as Philip said of
great Alexander his sonne Μακεδονία γάρ σ' οὐ χωρεῖ
[Macedonia is too small for you]. And specially vse

such games on horse-backe, as may teach you to
handle your armes thereon; such as the tilt, the ring,
and lowe-riding for handling of your sword.[5]
Basilikon Doron is interesting not only for setting
out the wide range of sports practised at a princely
level in Scotland, but also for its early advocacy of
the benefits of sport to health and the development
of skills. James's enthusiasm for horsemanship
in particular appears to correspond with the start
of racing in numerous burghs, which took up a
more formal encouragement of certain sports by
presenting trophies, such as silver bells for horse-
racing and silver arrows for archery. At Rattray in
Perthshire, the local minister, Silvester Rattray, is
thought to have gifted three trophies: a silver ball, a
silver arrow and a silver curling stone.[6] To the alarm
of the Puritan members of the House of Commons,
James VI and I also endorsed the widespread
participation in sports after church on Sundays
and other holy days in his 1618 proclamation, *The*
Book of Sports. James argued that Sundays and

View of the Tennis Court at Holyroodhouse, Edinburgh,
by James Gordon of Rothiemay, about 1647
National Library of Scotland, Edinburgh

The Holyroodhouse tennis court, marked as '51' in the
top left corner, stood to the south of Queen Mary's
Bath House on Abbeyhill, later served as a theatre and
concert hall, then as a weaver's workshop until it was
destroyed by fire in 1771.

festivals were the only days on which working
people, 'either men or women', could participate in
recreational activities to refresh their spirits and
exercise their bodies. Sport also appears to have
played an important part in school life. In 1636 in
order to make his teaching more relevant to his
pupils, the Master of Aberdeen Grammar School,
David Wedderburn, drew up a Latin *Vocabula*,
or vocabulary book, which included golfing,
bowling, football and archery terms.[7] By the early
seventeenth century the level of sporting activity,
especially in golf, began to sustain a relatively
substantial Scottish industry in manufacturing
specialist sporting equipment. For example,
in 1603 William Mayne, a 'bower, burgess in
Edinburgh', was appointed 'during all the days of
his lyf-time, master fledger [arrow-maker], bower
[longbow-maker], club-maker, and spier-maker
to his Hieness, alsweill for game as weir'. In 1618
James VI granted a twenty-one year monopoly in
Scotland to James Melville and William Berwick to
make and sell golf balls, and in 1635 the Edinburgh
bower Donald Blaine left 'clubheids and club-
schaftis ane thousand made and umade' on his
death.[8]

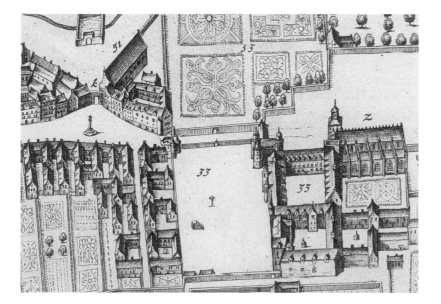

James VI's *Book of Sports* became an incendiary
document to Puritans when republished by his
son, Charles I, in 1633, contributing significantly
to the tumult in the build-up to the outbreak of the
Bishops' Wars of the 1630s and English Civil War in
the 1640s. Although not officially forbidden, Sunday
sport was decried by the Covenanters and not
encouraged under Oliver Cromwell's Protectorate,
as the gathering of crowds was conducive to all
sorts of sedition and plotting against the imposed
order. The pendulum swung the other way after the
Restoration of the horse-racing enthusiast, Charles
II, in 1660, when sporting activities began to flourish
again, and the associated problems of gambling and
drinking increased.

Royal tennis courts, or courtyards used for tennis
(for example Raploch House, Larkhall, Lanarkshire),
were probably still the most substantial structures
associated with sport at this period, but individuals
and some institutions were setting aside and laying
out grounds for other sports as noted in 1679 by
James Somerville:

The having of bowlling greenes, bulles for
archerie, tinnes-courts, and bullziart [billiards]
tables, in and about noblemen and gentlemen's
houses, is better by ffarre ffor manly exercize, then
to pass ther tyme in drinking, smocking tobacco,
ffingering of cards and tables.[9]

By far the most popular and fashionable outdoor
sporting facilities in the second half of the seventeenth century were private bowling greens, attached
to almost all the country houses of the nobility and
gentry.[10] Often the levelling of ground for bowling
was a significant achievement and expense in itself.
Many bowling greens were also sheltered by new
walls or sunk within a compartment of the garden.
Summerhouses frequently adjoined, or were located
close to, the bowling greens, perhaps marking
the initial development of a new building type, the
sporting pavilion – a place to store equipment and
where players took refreshments. The role of a
refreshment venue is implied by Patrick Lyon, 1st Earl
of Strathmore, when describing his new gatehouse to
the entrance court of Glamis Castle in the 1680s:

View of the Bowling Green and Summerhouse at Hatton House, Wilkieston, West Lothian, by John Slezer, about 1690
National Library of Scotland, Edinburgh

Bowling greens were common features of country houses by the late seventeenth century. In this engraving of Hatton House, the bowling green is shown on the left-hand side of the house. Adjoining the bowling green is a small building, which may have served as a summerhouse and/or a place for storing the bowls and serving refreshments to the bowlers.

... the gate house consists of on roume to the gardine and another to the bouling green, the walls are lined, the roof plaistered, the floor lay'd with black and whyt stone and are verie convenient and refreshful roumes to goe in to from the gardine and Bouling green.[11]

Increasing urbanisation and the rise of the mercantile and professional classes in the late seventeenth century had a profound impact on the development and spread of sport in Scotland. This is evidenced by the rapid expansion of the long game of golf, which by 1685 was being played in most of the major East Coast sea-trading burghs and in Kirkwall on Orkney.[12] Horse-racing too was a major sport, with races established from Lamberton (Berwick-upon-Tweed) and Dumfries in the south to Inverness, Banff and Huntly in the north. Perhaps the most significant sporting developments in this period were the formation of societies such as the curling society in Kinross dating from about 1667 and His Majesty's Company of Archers in Edinburgh in 1676, and the construction of communal facilities such as the bowling green at Haddington in 1662. Municipal encouragement for sports accompanied the growing wealth and power of the burghs, particularly in the form of prizes, such as the silver bells for horse-racing, silver arrows for archery, and even the twenty-shilling prize offered by Glasgow Town Council for the winner of a 'foot raice' on Glasgow Green in 1675.[13] By the late seventeenth century Leith could be considered the sporting capital of Scotland, with its wealth of venues for sports including horse-racing, archery, golf, bowling and tennis.

THE EIGHTEENTH CENTURY

The upheavals of the Jacobite Risings in the late seventeenth and early eighteenth centuries brought an influx of English troops, who introduced a new game, cricket, to the range of traditional Scottish sports. A group of Scottish aristocrats and gentry with connections to the fashionable London cricket clubs took to the sport enthusiastically in the later part of the eighteenth century. Also associated with the rise of military training was the sport of 'ornamental riding', which was practised in a large and 'by no means ornamental' building of 1764, known as the 'Royal Academy of Exercises', on the east side of Nicolson Street in Edinburgh.[14]

One of the key factors in the development of team sports was the codification of rules, setting out the dimensions of the field of play, number of players and governance of the game. This enabled teams to play under fair conditions in any location where the rules were adopted. The Company of Gentlemen Golfers in Edinburgh set out their 'Articles and Laws in Playing at Golf' in 1744, the same year as theStar and Garter Cricket Club of London established the first 'Laws of Cricket'. Another elite club that developed from the Star and Garter pub on Pall Mall, London, was the Jockey Club founded in 1750, which eventually came to codify the rules and regulate flat horse-racing throughout the UK. The Duddingston Curling Society adopted its influential Code of Curling Laws in 1806. By the end of the eighteenth century most codified sports were still relatively elite male-dominated activities for those with the leisure time to participate and the money to pay for the equipment, uniforms, subscriptions and compulsory weekly dining. Clubs and societies of all sorts proliferated in the late eighteenth and early nineteenth centuries, from legal, medical, military and philosophical to rather more eccentric societies, such as the Six Feet Club (1826), which encouraged gymnastic exercises for members over six feet in height.[15] The number of sporting societies increased significantly and the social side of sport had developed, but was mainly conducted in the existing taverns and hostelries of the towns, and still very few purpose-built facilities were constructed for sporting activity. These included a handful of 'golf houses' and Archers' Hall, which operated as commercial taverns; a small number of racecourse grandstands; and probably a few curling huts for storing curling stones.

THE NINETEENTH CENTURY

The Napoleonic Wars in the first two decades of the nineteenth century had a significant economic and social impact on Scotland, with a consequent decline in sporting activity. In 1815, after the Battle of Waterloo, there was the beginning of a resurgence in the popularity of sports, notably curling, and to a lesser degree golf, bowling, archery, skating, horse-racing, Highland games and cricket. Although the overcrowding of common lands had worsened in the late eighteenth and early nineteenth centuries as town populations swelled and non-sporting uses increased, the range of sports grew and included facilities such as horse-racing courses. The overcrowded common lands provided an incentive to subscription sporting clubs to find their own spaces, acquire their own properties and build their own facilities for storing equipment and socialising.

Technical developments helped the expansion of sports, and enabled them to be played more widely at relatively modest expense. Shallow artificial curling ponds, invented by John Cairnie in 1813, allowed curling to take place safely almost anywhere with a moderate water supply, and their fast-freezing qualities increased the number of playing days. The Gloucestershire engineer, Edwin Beard Budding of Stroud, invented the first hand-pushed lawnmower in 1827 and patented it in August 1830. However, it was the horse-drawn combined mower and roller, patented by Alexander Shanks of Arbroath in 1842, that really made possible the widespread availability of perfectly smooth playing surfaces for cricket, golf, croquet and bowls. James Leyland's steam-powered

mowers followed in 1893, then, from 1902 petrol engines became available commercially. Mowing machines were relatively slow to catch on in Scotland, as even up to the First World War many of the best greens were still hand-scythed and brushed.[16] Scottish groundsmen led the way in the use of sea-marsh turf over a drained foundation of clinker blinded with fine ash.[17] Sea-marsh turf was the toughest and smoothest naturally occurring grass playing surface. It was harvested from the marshes of the Solway Firth, the flats at the mouth of the River Irvine and later at Forres in Morayshire.[18] Advances in mechanised production created cheaper equipment to specified standards, such as circular polished granite curling stones in the first quarter of the nineteenth century and gutta percha golf balls from 1848 and later rubber-core golf balls from 1899.

Perhaps the most famous sporting patron of the nineteenth century was Archibald Montgomerie, 13th Earl of Eglinton, who, inspired by Walter Scott's *Ivanhoe* (1820), staged the extravagant romantic medieval re-enactment known as the Eglinton Tournament on 28 August 1839. The event attracted international attention from Rio de Janeiro to Kolkata, and a vast crowd of 100,000 people, many in medieval fancy-dress, made their way from the traffic-jammed roads of abandoned carriages and from the steamer pier at Ardrossan and the newly-opened railway station at Irvine to the tournament fields at Eglinton Castle. The provider of the knights' antique armour, Samuel Luke Pratt, designed a special tiltyard with stands to accommodate 2,000 people. Sadly the first day of spectacle was completely washed-out, with a thunder storm leaving a bedraggled cast of drenched maidens and rusty knights. It was another two days before everything dried out and a relatively successful tournament was held on Friday 30 August. The same romantic view of the medieval past seems to have prompted the earl to invest in the other ancient sports of Scotland and to encourage ritual and pageantry. In 1822 he established a racecourse at Bogside (Irvine), donated

→ Kays of Scotland Curling Stone Factory,
Barskimming Road, Mauchline, Ayrshire, about 1925
Photo: RCAHMS

Willie Cairns and 'Scottie' Wilson roughing out and
boring curling stones by hand. Founded in 1851, Kays
continue to have the exclusive right to harvest the finest
granite for curling stones from Ailsa Craig, and have
supplied stones to the Winter Olympics since 1924.

↓ *The Eglinton Tournament* by James Henry Nixon,
1839
East Ayrshire Council

prizes, and in 1839 staged the first steeplechase
in Scotland. Eglinton was instrumental in the
1828 revival of the Kilwinning papingo, a medieval
archery competition, and for some years he hosted
elaborate costumed archery competitions between
his Irvine Toxophilites and Glasgow teams.[19] In
the same year as the tournament, the earl began
construction of a rackets court with a great trussed
timber roof, which is now the oldest surviving
building for indoor sports in Scotland. Similarly
curling, bowling, golf and the more modern sports
of cricket, skating and yachting benefitted from
his patronage.

Although not a typical mainstream sporting
occasion, the Eglinton Tournament was the
first major spectator event of the railway age
in Scotland. Steam-powered transport was to
transform both participation in, and attendance
at, sporting events throughout the country. With
relative ease and moderate expense, a team or
an individual from one town or village could travel
beyond the confines of the burgh or parish to
compete, and larger crowds could gather to watch
events from far and wide. More mobile workforces
are thought to have brought sports with them, for
example the English textile workers of Hawick
and Selkirk and the papermill workers of Penicuik
founded cricket clubs in the 1840s and 1850s. The
advent of a new instant communication method, in
the form of the electric telegraph, proved helpful
in organising curling matches, where the depth
of the ice could be tested before a team set out.
Newspapers too began to use the telegraph to
report more quickly on a wider range of sports. The
Inverness Courier reported in December 1849 that
'Curling, that winter amusement so popular in the
south of Scotland, is getting rapidly into favour in
the north'.[20] By the end of the century, the railways
had helped to spread the curling craze to almost
every parish in Scotland. The spectacle of Highland
games also opened to Lowland visitors, encouraged by Queen Victoria's interest in the Braemar
Gathering. The rapid industrialisation that accompanied improved transport and communications

led to an enormous influx of people and wealth to
the cities and burghs, stimulating the creation of
middle class sporting clubs and societies with the
means to acquire and build their own facilities by
subscription. Patrons, like the Earl of Eglinton,
played an important role in advancing sport and
providing facilities and equipment for labourers and
factory workers. The landmark Factory Act of 1850
stipulated an end to work at 2pm on Saturdays,
for the first time allowing non-Sunday leisure for
factory workers. Schools and their former pupils'
associations also began to acquire their own sports
grounds, and to compete with other schools in the
mid century period.[21]

The continued growth in the professional and
mercantile classes, increased leisure time and
disposable income for some of the labouring
classes, better and more widespread education,
improved transport, a relatively stable and pros-
perous economy, cheaper mass-produced equipment, and a new concern with promoting public
health and exercise all contributed to the conditions
that led to an explosion of popular participation
and the birth of modern sports in the second half of
the nineteenth century. The rigorous disciplines of

sport were also considered beneficial to spiritual and moral well-being and social stability, providing healthy activity to those who might otherwise resort to crime, drunkenness and riot.[22] This was the period when many sporting clubs were formed and the construction of dedicated associated buildings really took off: clubhouses for golf; pavilions for croquet, tennis, bowls and cricket; huts for curling; stands and stadia for Highland games and football (incorporating tracks for athletics and cycling); grandstands for horse-racing; swimming pools; and gymnasia for gymnastics, badminton, boxing, wrestling, weight-lifting and fencing. Schools too began to incorporate physical education into the curriculum, renting or purchasing sports fields, first in the private sector and then in the public education system from the 1880s.[23]

From the 1850s new public parks were established and many of the burgh commons came to be managed formally in the manner of public parks by town councils. In Glasgow, for example, the town council began the purchase of lands to form Kelvingrove Park in 1852, and in about 1857 Glasgow Green was adopted as a public park.[24] The local Glasgow Public Parks Act of 1859 established funding for maintenance and development of the parks through levies and borrowing.[25] However,

the early new parks were laid out as ornamental gardens, with little or no provision for sports. Recognising the benefits of gymnastic exercise, the town council accepted the gift of an open-air gymnasium for Glasgow Green from the Manchester merchant, D.G. Fleming, in 1860.[26] Boxing also took place here. Cricket and football in particular were regarded as 'objectionable and even dangerous to most of the frequenters of the park'.[27] Golf was similarly hazardous in municipal parks. The City Improvement Acts of 1866 allowed Glasgow Town Council to purchase land specifically for recreation grounds. From 1866 the first of the new recreation grounds in Glasgow was gradually equipped with bowling greens, tennis courts and space for golf, football and cricket at Queen's Park, the birthplace of the Queen's Park Football Club. Private clubs, such as Queen's Park Bowling Club, rented ground from the town council and were responsible for laying out the field of play and constructing a clubhouse. But, it was not until the late 1880s and 1890s that demand for sporting venues forced town councils, and later the city corporations, to incorporate facilities into public parks. The sports of bowling and tennis were favoured as they required relatively small areas and simple facilities. Public demand played a part in private developments too,

for example at Hyndland in Glasgow, where the residents requested the inclusion of a bowling green at the heart of the new streets of upmarket tenements of the late 1890s.

Although the subscription clubs and societies of the larger burghs and cities had the means to construct pavilions and clubhouses, the enthusiasm for sports manifested itself almost anywhere that space could be found in the vicinity of smaller towns, villages, industrial complexes and agricultural estates. The slate workers of Cullipool (Highland games), fishermen of Tarbert (cricket), estate workers at Largie Castle (cricket), foundry workers at Monifieth (golf), estate workers at Ballikinrain (football), paper mill workers of Penicuik (cricket), shopkeepers and merchants of Newmilns (bowling), excise officers at the Bladnoch Distillery (cricket), inhabitants of Crawfordjohn (curling), mill workers of Hawick (cricket) and villagers of Doune (quoiting) are just some of the thousands of local teams that played recreational sport without sophisticated facilities or equipment.[28]

Glasgow Green Outdoor Gymnasium, 1860
Photo: RCAHMS

Recognising the benefits of gymnastic exercise, the town council accepted the gift of an open-air gymnasium for Glasgow Green from the Manchester merchant, D.G. Fleming, in 1860. Boxing also took place here.

The Eglinton Tournament had heralded the beginning of mass-spectator events in the 1830s, but the rapid growth and phenomenal success of association football in the last quarter of the nineteenth century transformed popular sport in Scotland. The world's first international football match between Scotland and England was staged in Glasgow in 1872. The fixture and the feverish reporting in the press fuelled the excitement and interest in the sport. A new suburban building type, the football stadium, grew out of the sudden need to accommodate tens of thousands of spectators in the cities and towns. In particular, Queen's Park Football Club in Glasgow was a pioneer in constructing new stands and terraces at each of their three Hampden grounds. Part of their success

The Royal Patent Gymnasium, Canonmills,
Edinburgh, 1864–5
Photo: RCAHMS

This extravagant outdoor gymnasium constructed on the site of Canonmills Loch was the creation of John Cox of Gorgie House, a businessman and philanthropist. Part funfair and part gymnasium, the many machines and contraptions had the serious purpose of the 'promotion of healthful and exhilarating exercise'. Apart from an indoor gymnasium containing traditional gymnastic equipment, there was *a vast 'rotary boat', 471 feet in circumference, seated for 600 rowers; a 'giant see-saw', named 'Chang', 100 feet long and 7 feet broad, supported on an axle, and capable of containing 200 persons, alternately elevating them to a height of 50 feet, and then sinking them almost to the ground; a 'velocipede paddle merry-go-round', 160 feet in circumference, seated for 600 persons, who propel the machine by sitting astride on the rim, and push their feet against the ground; a 'self-adjusting trapeze', in five series of three each, enabling gymnasts to swing by the hands 130 feet from one trapeze to the other; a 'compound pendulum', capable of holding about 100 persons, and kept in motion by their own exertions.* The Gymnasium was hugely successful, and remained the 'New Wonder of Edinburgh' until its closure at the end of the nineteenth century.

grew from an increasing commercialism, charging entrance fees in order to develop the grounds and stands. Although Queen's Park jealously guarded their amateur position, other clubs quickly embraced professional status. On the back of his experience designing Rugby Park for Kilmarnock and the second Ibrox Stadium for Rangers in 1899, the Glaswegian Archibald Leitch went on to become the most prolific and sought-after stadium architect and engineer in the UK in the early years of the twentieth century. Crowd management and safety were now factors in the design of sporting buildings. At a local level, the game caught on quickly in schools, and hundreds of junior and senior clubs soon started up across the country. Golf and curling also attracted huge numbers of new players and clubs were established throughout the country. The first Open Championship in golf was played at Prestwick in 1860. The game made young Tom Morris Scotland's first sporting star of the modern era, after winning four consecutive Open titles between 1868 and 1873 (the championship was not held in 1871).

← Alloa Baths Gymnasium, Primrose Street,
Alloa, 1898
Listed Category A
Photo: RCAHMS

Friedrich Ludwig Jahn constructed the first gymnasium
of the modern era in Prussia in 1811, equipped with
parallel and horizontal bars and pommel and vaulting
horses. A 'fencing gymnasium' was established in
West Nile Street, Glasgow, from 1824. From the 1860s
a number of outdoor and commercial indoor gymnasia
were built in the larger towns and cities.

↙ A game of croquet at Sand Lodge, Leebotten,
Shetland, late nineteenth century.
Private Collection

↓ Shinty at Ballachulish, 1920s?
Glencoe and North Lorn Folk Museum

The period was remarkable not only for the
sudden success of football, golf and curling, but
also for a range of other new or newly codified
sports that flourished, with the consequent formation of facilities and clubs. In November 1856 the
toy-maker Isaac Spratt registered the rules of
croquet with the Stationers' Company in London.
Spratt also published the earliest pamphlet
describing badminton in 1860. Croquet was probably being played in Scotland by December 1859,
when James Hogg's Bazaar in West Register
Street, Edinburgh, advertised croquet amongst the
'newest games' available as Christmas presents
and New Year gifts.[29] David Johnstone Macfie, a
sugar refiner of Greenock won the first Scottish
Championship, held on the Beechgrove Croquet
Greens, Moffat, on 18 August 1870.[30] Like many
early croquet venues, the Beechgrove Croquet
Greens lasted only a few years before they were
adapted for the even newer sport of lawn tennis.
Boxing with gloves was first conducted under
the Marquess of Queensberry's rules in 1867. The
older handling form of football, rugby, set up its
own governing body, the Scottish Football Union,
in 1873. William Wilson, manager of the Victoria
Baths Club in Glasgow, developed the rules of
water polo from 1877.[31] In shinty, Strathglass Shinty
Club of Cannich (Comunn Camanachd Straghlais)
is considered to be the oldest constituted club,
dating from 1879. The modern rules of the game
were established in a match between Strathglass
and Glenurquhart at Bught Park, Inverness on 12
February 1887. Although there was a long tradition
of athletic competition in Scotland, including the
Red Hose Race at Carnwath (dating from at least
1456), the annual sports days of the big football
clubs brought it a significant following.[32] The
Scottish Amateur Athletic Association was formed
on 26 February 1883, and the first championship
meeting took place at Powderhall Stadium in
Edinburgh on 23 June of the same year.[33] The creation of the Scottish Amateur Swimming Association
took place in 1888. Ten hockey clubs came together
to establish the Scottish Hockey Association on 18
November 1901, five years after the formation of the
first Scottish hockey club, Clackmannan County.
Women's lacrosse in Scotland dates back to 1890
at St Leonards School in St Andrews, where the
headmistress Louisa Lumsden introduced the sport
after watching a men's lacrosse game between the
Canghuwaya Indians and the Montreal Lacrosse
Club.[34]

Companies that specialised in prefabricated
sporting buildings emerged in the second half

of the nineteenth century, like Fred Braby & Co. of London, 'contractors for pavilions, stands, barricades and requisites for football and cricket enclosures', who set up their Eclipse Works in Glasgow in 1875 to cope with Scottish demand. Such structures could be transported to any part of the country by train and erected by local joiners. Other companies specialised in fixtures, such as W.T. Ellison & Co. of Salford, who supplied patent 'rush preventive turnstiles' to most of the large Scottish football clubs from 1895, allowing clubs to count the number of spectators and tally them with the sums collected by the stilesmen. Paterson & Calvert of Glasgow, asphalters and cement paviors, developed a specialism as curling pond contractors in the 1880s. The Ayrshire-born John Boyd Dunlop's invention of the first inflatable rubber tyre in 1887 transformed the technology of cycling. Newspapers, magazines, journals and books all contributed to growing expertise, not just in the playing of sports, but also in the manufacture and marketing of equipment and the construction of pitches and facilities.

Although women had long played sports including golf, swimming, curling, bowling, archery, skating and football, and had participated in boxing on Glasgow Green as far back as 1828, the sporting

After Charles Rennie Mackintosh *Design for a Golf Clubhouse*, **about 1910**
Hunterian Art Gallery and Museum, University of Glasgow

This design for a golf clubhouse in an unknown location was found amongst Charles Rennie Mackintosh's possessions at his death in 1928. Although the drawing is not by Mackintosh, it does exhibit stylistic similarities with his work of about 1910, such as the attic addition to the Glasgow School of Art of 1907–9. The familiar veranda of a traditional single storey clubhouse is present, but in most other respects, the design is innovative, with white roughcast, flat roofs, deep eaves and large areas of square-pane glazing in a Japanese manner. The building appears not to have been constructed.

clubs remained almost exclusively male until the 1860s. Even then, women's clubs were usually relegated to use of shared facilities at off-peak hours, or exiled to inferior facilities. Very few sports accommodated mixed-sex teams until well into the twentieth century, although on private grounds, family games of curling and bowls are recorded before 1850.[35] In the 1890s the first women's golf clubs began to acquire their own properties and to build their own clubhouses. The Scottish Ladies' Golfing Association led the way in establishing a governing body for the women's sport in 1904.

Ralston Community Sports Centre, Penilee Road, Paisley, 1937, designed by Harry Cook of Cook & Hamilton
Listed Category A
Photo: Historic Scotland, Edinburgh

THE TWENTIETH CENTURY

The huge range of social, economic and technological factors that influenced the construction of sporting buildings in the twentieth century can only be touched on here. By the beginning of the century numerous landed estates were under considerable financial pressure from low land rental values and high labour costs, and the traditional patronage of local sporting venues, sites and competitions was under threat. The enormous disruption caused by the First World War exacerbated the situation, but wealthier golf clubs and entrepreneurs took advantage of depressed land values after the war to acquire sites for golf courses and sporting resorts, such as Gleneagles. As the country recovered, new building materials and technologies transformed what was possible in the construction of sporting buildings, cars and buses broadened their availability, and more leisure time and a better understanding of health and welfare encouraged their use. Town councils and city corporations increasingly assumed the sporting patronage role previously occupied by local landowners, vying with each other to provide facilities, like the Portobello Pool wave machine, that would draw residents and day-trippers alike.

The first modern-day Olympic Games took place in the Panathenaic Stadium in Athens in 1896, the first Winter Olympics was hosted in Chamonix in 1924, the first Fifa World Cup played in Uruguay in 1930, and Hamilton, Ontario, hosted the inaugural Commonwealth (originally 'British Empire') Games in the same year. Although government encouraged sport for reasons of social cohesion, stability and health after the First World War, it was undoubtedly the globalisation of sports, and particularly home team success on the international stage that had an immediate inspirational effect on the popularity of sports and the need for facilities. The spectacular last-minute triumph of the Great Britain ice hockey team over the Canadians at the 1936 Winter Olympic Games at Garmisch-Partenkirchen led to a frenzy of ice rink building across Scotland. The Inter-war years saw astonishing attendance figures for football matches, with the 149,415 official crowd at the Scotland-England international match at Hampden on 17 April 1937 still standing as a European record. Swimming too attracted enormous summer crowds: the outdoor pool at Portobello recorded 9,160 spectators and 5,241 bathers, who queued for an hour-and-a-half for tickets, bringing the daily total of visitors to 14,401 on 25 July 1937.[36]

Sir Chris Hoy Velodrome, 1000 London Road,
Glasgow, 2009–12
Photo: Keith Hunter

Designed by 3D Reid with Sports Concept, the Sir
Chris Hoy Velodrome was built alongside the Emirates
Arena as the only new sporting complex for the 2014
Commonwealth Games.

Scottish greenkeepers maintained their pre-eminence in the construction and maintenance of playing surfaces during the first half of the twentieth century. Influential greenkeepers, such as William Paul of Paisley, produced numerous manuals and articles on the subject in the 1920s. In the same period, scientific research into turf, ferti-lisers and pesticides, along with new turf production companies, seed certification and cheaper seeded soil surfaces ended the traditional dominance of Scottish sea-marsh turf for greens after the Second World War.[37] The inter-war years were relatively conservative for sporting architecture in Scotland, with little money or appetite for the adventurous structural and engineering projects that were beginning to emerge internationally, such as Carlos Arnicjes and Martin Dominguez' sculptural concrete racecourse stand of 1934 at the Hipódromo la Zarzuela in Madrid.

The Second World War had a significant and long-lasting impact on sporting buildings and spaces. Although new facilities were erected rapidly for military training purposes, no new civilian sporting buildings were constructed, many existing buildings were mothballed, and parks and sports pitches were transformed into allotments as part of the 'Dig for Victory' campaign. In the post-war rebuilding programme, sporting buildings were not a government priority, and many sporting clubs had difficulty in obtaining permits for building materials to repair damaged or neglected buildings and playing areas. In spite of the lack of facilities, many sports continued to thrive. The growth of broadcasting, in particular television from the 1950s, had an enormous impact on sport, on the public demand for sports facilities, and on the economics of sport, ushering in an era of commercialisation and the expansion of professional sport.[38]

When the building of sporting venues eventually resumed on any scale, local authorities provided many of the new facilities. Most favoured new 'sports arenas', 'sports centres' or 'leisure centres' over disparate facilities for individual sports, for reasons of cost and ease of maintenance. Individual clubs too began the process of post-war renewal. Many bowling and golf clubs, for example, sought to extend or replace existing clubhouses with larger social spaces and improved changing facilities. The emphasis on speed of construction, price, low-maintenance and the equipping of buildings resulted in relatively few new sporting buildings of high architectural quality before 1980. Where the various schools of the Modern Movement (typified by use of modern materials, clear structural expression, simplified geometric forms, and primacy given to the function of the building) had widespread influence on Scotland's social housing and commercial and industrial architecture of the 1950s to 1970s, it failed to gain much of a hold in the more conservative field of sporting buildings. There were some obvious exceptions, including the Dam Park Stadium stand (1963) in Ayr, the Gala Fairydean stand (1964) in Galashiels, the Dollan Baths (1968) in East Kilbride, and the Royal Commonwealth Pool (1970) in Edinburgh, which are all now listed buildings. In football, the second Ibrox disaster in 1971 prompted the Safety of Sports Grounds Act of 1975, which applied across the UK. Although no Scottish legislation followed the Taylor Report after the 1989 Hillsborough disaster, the Scottish Premier League made all-seater stadia a condition of membership in 1998 (since relaxed in 2011). Most of the league clubs had begun work towards all-seater stadia before 1998 – the Dons had pioneered the all-seater stadium in the UK at Pittodrie in 1978, and Rangers introduced a new generation of safety and comfort-oriented stadia with the redevelopment of Ibrox in 1978–81.[39] Top-level sport became big business in the 1980s. Sponsorship, television rights, commercial activities, maximised ticket receipts, hospitality, supporters' clubs, diversification of building use, catering, special events, media relations and marketing became essential to sporting concerns, from football and rugby to horse-racing and golf. By the 1990s even sports that had cherished their amateur status, such as rugby union, removed restrictions on professional players. The technology associated with sporting

venues and equipment, and the science of sport and sports medicine, progressed in leaps and bounds. At the same time the design of new and refurbished sporting buildings changed to incorporate higher levels of comfort for players and spectators, better catering facilities, improved accessibility, energy efficiency, and advances in safety and services.

THE TWENTY-FIRST CENTURY

The beginning of the twenty-first century has seen a renaissance in Scotland's sporting buildings. In many cases the investment of funding from the National Lottery and the Scottish Government through sportscotland has enabled projects that would not previously have been possible. The Community Amateur Sports Club Scheme of 2002 was an important measure that enabled grass roots clubs to benefit from a range of tax reliefs. Increasingly, collaborative partnerships are delivering state-of-the-art regional facilities, such as the new sports villages in Stirling, Aberdeen and Ravenscraig, and community sports hubs. In some places, for example the Commonwealth Games venues in the East End of Glasgow, the siting of top-class sporting facilities has been used to encourage investment and regeneration of surrounding areas. High-quality designs now respond not only to the needs of the people who use them and to the character of the places in which they are located, but to a raft of accessibility, engineering, material,

technical, technological, servicing, safety, maintenance and environmental requirements and possibilities. These factors are apparent both in refurbishments, like the Royal Commonwealth Pool in Edinburgh (S & P Architects with Buro Happold, 2012), and in new buildings such as the Balornoch Bowling Club (studiokap, 2005), Campbeltown Aqualibrium (Page\Park, 2006), Stirling County Cricket Club (jmarchitects, 2007), Mull and Iona Swimming Pool (Crerar & Partners, 2008), Playsport Golf at East Kilbride (Smith Design Associates, 2009), Stirling Sports Village (S & P Architects, 2009) Aberdeen Sports Village (Reiach and Hall, 2009), Ravenscraig Regional Sports Facility (Populous Architects with Buro Happold, 2010), Broxburn United Sports Club (Slorach Wood Architects, 2011), Michael Woods Sport and Leisure Centre in Glenrothes (B3/Cre8 Architects, 2011), Kirkcaldy Leisure Centre (B3/Cre8 Architects, 2013) and the various new and refurbished facilities for the Glasgow 2014 Commonwealth Games including the Emirates Arena and Sir Chris Hoy Velodrome (3D Reid with Sports Concept, 2009–12) and Tollcross Aquatics Centre (Glasgow City Council, 2011–13).

Archery

ARCHERS' HALL, 66 BUCCLEUCH STREET, EDINBURGH, 1776
Listed Category A

The social and administrative activities of the Royal Company of Archers took place in local taverns until Archers' Hall was built in Buccleuch Street to designs by Alexander Laing in 1776–7. Laing was a significant architect, responsible for the construction of the South Bridge (1786–8) in Edinburgh, Inverness Tolbooth steeple (1789) and Darnaway Castle (1802–12) in Morayshire, amongst numerous other projects.

**Apollo! Patron of the Lyre,
And of the valiant Archers' bow,
Me with such sentiments inspire
As may appear from thee to flow,
When by thy special will and dread command,
I sing the merits of the Royal Band.**

Allan Ramsay, on his appointment as Bard to the Royal Company of Archers in 1743[1]

An Act of Parliament of 1424 required the establishment of bow-butts on every piece of land worth more than £10, particularly near churches, so that all men over the age of twelve could practise archery on Sundays and feast days.[2] Similar Acts followed under James II, James IV and James V, in which 'wapenshawings' (showing of weapons) were required. Many old burghs retain street names such as 'Bow Butts' or 'Butts Wynd' that reflect the former location of these longbow practice areas, a number of which survived into the nineteenth century. The annual Kilwinning Papingo (popinjay, or painted bird) tournament, in which a wooden pigeon is dislodged from the tower of Kilwinning Abbey by almost vertical shooting of arrows, is thought to date back to the foundation of the Ancient Society of Kilwinning Archers in 1483. Irvine too had a papingo competition. Mary, Queen of Scots, is reputed to have practised the sport in the gardens of Falkland Palace in the 1560s, and an inventory of her possessions mentions a velvet glove used when shooting.[3] By the seventeenth century, longbows had fallen out of use as a military weapon, but target archery continued as a recreation: many towns, such as Musselburgh, Peebles and Selkirk, and also the University of St Andrews, held archery competitions for the prize of a silver arrow. In 1774 James Cant recorded the existence of large ancient stones on the South Inch of Perth, which were thought to mark the position of the targets at a rather improbable distance of over 500 fathoms (914 metres).[4] Certainly in the last quarter of the eighteenth century, the sport was gaining in popularity and fashionability, as reflected by the Royal Company of Archers' acquisition of a hall and

Robert and Ronald Ferguson of Raith, 'The Archers',
by Sir Henry Raeburn, about 1790
The National Gallery, London

Sir Henry Raeburn became a member of the Royal
Company of Archers in 1791. Fellow archers formed the
subjects of two of his greatest paintings, Dr Nathaniel
Spens (1793) and the young brothers Robert and Ronald
Ferguson of Raith (about 1790). The Royal Company
admitted Robert as a member in 1792, and Ronald
followed in 1801.

ARCHERS' HALL,
66 BUCCLEUCH STREET, EDINBURGH, 1776
Listed Category A

Although it has much older origins, 'His Majesty's
Company of Archers' was formally constituted to revive
the ancient skill of archery in 1676. Queen Anne granted
a royal charter in 1703, establishing the company as the
Royal Company of Archers. At this point, the company's
butts of turf or straw appear to have been set up in
the yard of a tavern. Two permanent new butts were
constructed to the west of Parliament House in 1713,
and these remained the favourite practice ground until
Thomas Hope of Rankeillour offered land at Hope Park,
now The Meadows, in 1726. The new butts, just to the
south of George Square, were of considerable expense,
planted round about with holly, yew and lime trees, and
eventually enclosed with a stone wall.

Like the contemporary 'golf houses', Archers' Hall
was intended to operate commercially as a tavern, with
precedence given to use by the Royal Company. The
original three-bay building comprised a 40-ft by 23-ft
hall with a gallery, two bar-rooms, two parlours and two
or three bedrooms and a kitchen. There was a bowling
green behind the hall. Covered butts were constructed
behind the hall in 1790, and in 1813 the residents of
Buccleuch Place petitioned to have the now ruinous
open-air butts removed from The Meadows. The
Royal Company lobbied successfully to provide the
personal bodyguard for the lavish ceremonial visit of
George IV to Edinburgh in 1822, and have served as the
Sovereign's Bodyguard in Scotland since that date.

After a financially disappointing period as a tavern,
the hall was managed directly by the Royal Company
from 1826. Throughout the nineteenth century there
were numerous deliberations about how to reconfigure
the hall in a more convenient manner. It was 1899
before Arthur Forman Balfour Paul was selected to
expand the building. Balfour Paul designed a southern
extension in contrasting sandstone, which contains
a grand staircase to the old hall on the first floor. The
interior was almost entirely remodelled with panelling
and ornate plasterwork cornices. The old east-facing
windows of the hall were blocked to allow display of
the Royal Company of Archers' magnificent portrait
collection, and a decoratively carved porch was added
to the main entrance. Ldn Architects designed the new
glazed extension and practice range in 2008. The Royal
Company of Archers still play for the Musselburgh
Arrow. Dating from at least 1603, it is believed to be one
of the oldest archery trophies in the world.

in the portraits of archers by Sir Henry Raeburn.

Thanks in large part to the *Waverley* novels
of Sir Walter Scott, there was a huge revival of
interest in romantic Scottish traditions and history
in the early nineteenth century, from which archery
profited. Societies, such as the Irvine Toxophilites
(1814), Zingari Archers, Dalry, Saltcoats, St Mungo
and Kinning Park Archery Clubs all flourished in the
west of Scotland, and the Salisbury Archers' Club
(1836) and Edinburgh Toxophilites (1858) developed in the east of Scotland.[5] A Scottish National
Archery Meeting was held annually in the first half
of the nineteenth century, with York Rounds (6
dozen arrows at 100 yards, 4 dozen arrows at 80
yards and 2 dozen arrows at 60 yards) shot by the
men and National Rounds (4 dozen arrows at 60
yards, and 2 dozen at 50 yards) shot by the women.
The most popular of these meetings took place in
1858 at Eglinton Castle, the home of Scotland's
keenest sporting earl. By 1875 there were a number
of women's clubs, including the Edinburgh Ladies'
Archery Club (1867), partly encouraged by Queen
Victoria's enthusiasm for the sport.[6]

Numerous local and university clubs were
founded, or re-founded after the Second World
War, as interest in the ancient sport revived. The
Burntisland, Dundee, Edinburgh Ladies, and Troon
Archery Clubs and the Ettrick Bowmen, Glasgow
Archers, Kilwinning Society of Archers and the
Royal Company of Archers formed the Scottish
Archery Association in March 1949. There are now
over fifty clubs or societies active in Scotland.
The British Long-Bow Society has four affiliated
longbow-only clubs in Scotland: Green Hollow
Bowmen (1996), Lorn Longbows (2004), Highland
Longbows (1995) and Ettrick Forest Archers
(2007).

The hall at
Archers' Hall
Photo: RCAHMS

Café Royal,
Edinburgh.
Painted glass
window by
Ballantine &
Gardiner, about
1900
Photo: RCAHMS

Royal Company
of Archers tartan
uniform of about
1750

National Museums
of Scotland,
Edinburgh

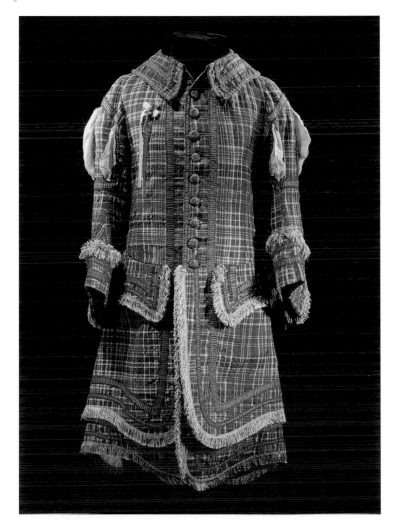

Bowling and Skittles

Mr D. Ferguson designed the Burntisland Bowling Club Pavilion for the Burntisland Recreation Company. It was opened on 2 August 1893 and cost £300. Initially the pavilion also serviced the three tennis courts that lay to the north. The bowling green itself had been opened in July 1892.

Every county town was provided with a public bowling-green for the diversion of the inhabitants in the summer evenings. All classes were represented among the players, and it was usual for persons of different ranks to take part in the same game. A bowling-green usually formed part of the policy or pleasure grounds of country houses. At these private bowling-greens ladies also shared in the amusement, thus rendering it greatly more attractive.

Thomas Somerville, Minister of Jedburgh, about 1814[1]

It is impossible to trace a single origin for the ancient sport of bowling, but the modern game of flat green bowls, as played throughout the world, is shaped by its development in Scotland from the sixteenth to the nineteenth centuries. Like its winter cousin, curling, bowls has a long tradition of widespread participation across social classes and gender. Numerous variants existed before the nineteenth century, including 'lang bowlis' or bulleting (distance road-bowling towards a defined target), pennystanes (flat, round stones thrown at a target on the ground), rowbowllis (rolled bowls), allay bowlis (alley bowls on a surface of clay, sand or grass towards a feather marker), and kyles (skittles).[2] The earliest reference to any form of the sport in Scotland is thought to be in April 1497 when James IV played 'lang bowlis' at St Andrews.[3] An Act of Edinburgh Town Council in 1581 banned the playing of 'bowling in yairdis' on the sabbath.[4] James VI created a bowling green in the ruins of Dunfermline Abbey in about 1596. Henry Adamson referred to his friend James Gall's 'alley bowles' in his poem The Muses Threnodie of 1620.[5] Glazing estimates for Dunfermline Palace in 1654 refer to the dismantling of 'the wark callit the kylspell', probably an indoor skittles alley created for Anne of Denmark.[6] Royal enthusiasm for bowling certainly had an impact on the widespread adoption of the game by the nobility and gentry throughout the seventeenth century. Almost no towerhouse or prestigious townhouse was complete without its

William Adam designed surely the grandest of bowling greens and pavilions for the Hamilton Palace estate of James, 5th Duke of Hamilton and 2nd Duke of Brandon, in 1732. The primary purpose of the magnificent Chatelherault buildings (named after a former family title) was as a hunting lodge for the duke and his guests, but the raised central compartment of the rear gardens appears to have been laid out as a bowling green from the start. Jokingly described by Adam as 'The Dogg Kennell att Hamilton', the hunting lodge formed the spectacular skyline climax of a 1.5-mile axial avenue from Hamilton Palace.

bowling green. The greens were rectangular plots of levelled and smooth grass, usually in a sheltered location close to the house, as for example at the old towerhouse of Arniston in Midlothian.[7] Garden buildings and summerhouses were often sited near to the bowling greens, and perhaps served as early pavilions. The first public bowling green in Scotland was laid out in 1662 beside the Nungate Bridge at Haddington as recorded in the minutes of the town council of 18 August 1662:

The samyne day the provest, baillies, counsel and deacons of the said Burgh, efter mature deliberation, ordainit Wm. Allan merchant burges, ye late Treasurer to the Kirk Sessioun, to delyver and give up to Patrick Young a sum of Scottis money for building of ane house at and wall aboot and laying the groond of ane bowilling grein on the sandis of the said Burgh.[8]

The appearance of the bowling green house is not known, but it was later used as part of the set for a play performed by the pupils of the grammar school.[9] The College at St Andrews built a bowling green in 1685, and there was certainly one in use at King's College, Aberdeen, by 1689.[10] Glasgow Town Council sold land in the Candleriggs to Mungo Cochrane for a commercial public bowling green in 1695, which was described as 'necessary for the ornament of the town and good and conveniency of the inhabitants'.[11] Similarly there were commercial bowling greens in Edinburgh and Leith.

Enthusiasm for bowling continued and grew during the eighteenth century. As the century progressed, the provision of bowling greens shifted away from the private individual towards more communal, commercial and institutional facilities. This shift was partly a consequence of the rising mercantile and professional middle classes and their development of societies and clubs, and partly a matter of gardening fashion for the nobility and gentry, as the taste for compartmental formal gardens waned and landscape and picturesque gardens took their place. Institutions, such as Cowane's Hospital (almshouse) in Stirling and Heriot's Hospital (school) in Edinburgh, laid out bowling greens.[12] The minutes of Cowane's Hospital contain the earliest record of the use of sea-marsh turf when the green was re-laid in 1738.[13] The first bowling club in Scotland was formed at Haddington in 1709. Kilmarnock Bowling Club, the oldest continuously active bowling club in the country, was instituted in 1740 and played on a large green to the north of the Cross. Edinburgh Town Council granted a Seal of Cause to the Edinburgh Society of Bowlers in 1769, establishing them as an official entity, governed by their own seventeen 'Regulations relative to the Exercise of Bowling'.[14] A merchant, William Tod, presented a silver jack to the society in May 1771.[15] The 'jack' or 'kitty' is the smaller ball at which the bowls are aimed. The annual winner of the silver jack attached a medal to what is now the oldest surviving trophy in the sport. Most of the forty-one founder members were merchants or professional men, including lawyers and accountants, who played on refurbished greens at Heriot's Hospital.[16]

The early clubs relied on entrance fees and yearly subscriptions for ground rental, green construction and maintenance, so remained relatively elite institutions. Exceptions could be found where landowners extended their patronage, notably William Harley, who included a bowling green in his pleasure grounds in Glasgow, and the Earl of Eglinton, who established bowling greens in all the villages on his estates.[17] A parallel sport, which enjoyed a more widespread working class following in the nineteenth century, was quoiting (pronounced 'kiting'). Quoiting took place in summer and involved throwing heavy metal rings of between 8 lbs (3.6 kg) and 12 lbs (5.5 kg) over a peg, usually over a distance of 22 yards (20 metres). Often the quoiting rinks were beside pubs.

James Brown's *Manual of Bowling* of 1892 identifies the 1840s as the period when bowling really began to expand in popularity as a result of increasing wealth and improving living conditions, health and education.[18] Glasgow in particular enjoyed a groundswell of popular support for lawn bowling. There were four clubs in the city before

1840, fifteen by 1864, and twenty-three listed in Brown's 1892 manual.

In 1864 William Wallace Mitchell, a Glasgow cotton merchant, drew up his *Manual of Bowl-Playing, Containing Laws and Rules of the Game*, which forms the basis of all subsequent bowling laws. Thomas Taylor Ltd of Glasgow invented and patented a machine for manufacturing bowls with a standardised bias in 1871. 'Bias' is achieved by shaping the inner edge of the bowl, and causes the curve in the path of the bowl. The bowls were made of *lignum vitae*, the 'wood of life', an extraordinarily strong, tough, dense and impervious self-lubricating wood, native to the West Indies, parts of Central America and northern South America.[19] Mitchell estimated that by 1882 there were 364 bowling clubs throughout Scotland. The first national bowling association in the world, the Scottish Bowling Association, was formed in 1892. The newly formed International Bowling Board adopted the Scottish Bowling Association's rules of the game and the Thomas Taylor standard bowl as the minimum bias bowl for all international matches from 1928.

The decades straddling 1900 saw the peak of bowling pavilion construction. Sometimes in conjunction with tennis courts, sometimes just serving bowling greens, most pavilions of the period adopted a rustic, picturesque outward appearance, often with an Arts and Crafts character. Tennis and bowling pavilions were often combined in middle class areas. With the odd exceptions, such as the two storey Co-operative bowling pavilion in Alloa and the Braid and Whitehouse and Grange pavilions in Edinburgh, most bowling pavilions were designed as single storey structures, often symmetrical with a gable or pediment over the door. Verandas for shelter were also a common feature.

The tradition of locating bowling greens as focal features of housing developments continued in the many local authority 'Homes for Heroes' schemes that sprang up after the First World War, such as Andrew David Haxton's Scoonie Crescent in Leven, Fife, of 1919. Elsewhere in cities, bowling and tennis clubs were occasionally built in the spaces left over when the tenement builders moved on, e.g. Dowanhill and Partickhill in Glasgow. Provision of recreational facilities was a key element in the Garden City movement, on whose principles many of the inter-war local authority housing schemes were based. As the popularity of quoiting dwindled in agricultural, industrial and mining communities, so bowls acquired a new following. The Miners' Welfare Fund was set up under the provisions of

Ardgowan Club Pavilion, Ardgowan Square,
Greenock, 1924
Listed Category B
Photo: Photo: Historic Scotland, Edinburgh

Meigle Bowling Club Pavilion, Dundee Road,
Meigle, 1897
Listed Category B

Bowling Pavilion, Duthie Park, Aberdeen, 1899
Listed Category C

Aberdeen Town Council's Links and Parks Committee
selected a design by the City Architect, John Rust, in
March 1899 for a 'building of wood, with slated roof,
containing verandah, dressing rooms (fitted up with
boxes for balls and racquets), lavatory accommodation
etc.' at an estimated cost of £245. In 1922 the town
council altered the pavilion to cater for a new bowling
green and five public tennis courts with blaise surfaces
on the adjacent ground. The pavilion was refurbished
for use by the Duthie Park Ranger Service in 2013.

the Mining Industry Act 1920 in the interests of
'the social well-being, recreation and conditions of
living of workers in or about coalmines'. Numerous
bowling greens and pavilions were established
between the 1920s and 1950s through the Welfare
Fund in connection with welfare institutes or
halls. Like most other types of sporting building,
the bowling pavilion remained largely conservative in design throughout the twentieth century.
However, there are rare inter-war examples of more
adventurous architectural approaches, such as
the bowling and tennis pavilion at King George's
Park, Carnwath, designed in 1935 for the local
authority by J.H. Fraser Stewart in the flat-roofed,
geometric International Style. Touches of flat-
roofed Modernism can be seen in the grandest of
the inter-war pavilions at Queen's Park in Glasgow,
designed by John Balantine in 1929 and extended
by an annexe in 1938.[20]

The small size of many of the nineteenth-century
bowling pavilions frequently resulted in extensions
and alterations, such as the infilling or glazing of
the verandas, in the mid to later twentieth century
as bowling clubs grew to accommodate bars and
function rooms. From the outset, isolated pavilions
have been vulnerable to burglary and vandalism,
sometimes resulting in destruction through fire.
There are no listed bowling pavilions from the post-
Second World War period of the twentieth century.
The current generation of architects is breathing
new life into the pavilion form in buildings such as
the Balornock Bowling Club pavilion, designed by
studiokap in 2005.[21]

DUNFERMLINE BOWLING CLUB, PRIORY LANE, DUNFERMLINE, 1895
Listed Category C

The club was established in 1852 by a group of twelve local artisans and tradesmen. Making use of an area of garden ground at the top of Woodhead Street, the game became popular so quickly that members of the public who used the green were ordered to pay for green maintenance as a penalty. The club moved to a new and larger green at Priory Lane in 1861. A 'rustic' clubhouse was built the following year. In 1895 Thomas Hyslop Ure designed the present club pavilion, which was constructed for £354.

A Game of Bowls by John Muir Wood, about 1845, is one of the earliest photographs of bowling
National Galleries of Scotland, Edinburgh

Café Royal, Edinburgh. Painted glass window by Ballantine & Gardiner, about 1900

The Silver Jacks of the Edinburgh Society of Bowlers, presented as a prize by the merchant William Tod in 1771. Winners attached medals to the trophy.
National Museums of Scotland, Edinburgh

The skittles alley dates from 1880, although an earlier alley stood on the site. The Trotters Club, founded in 1882, is thought to be the world's oldest active skittles club, and still meets at the Sheep Heid on the first Saturday of the month. Skittles is played in a similar way to tenpin bowling, but with some fundamental differences. The wooden ball is released using both hands on a shorter lane, either from a standing position or by launching the body on to the alley. The double-handed release removes the requirement for finger holes in the ball.

Cricket

GRANGE CRICKET CLUB PAVILION, PORTGOWER PLACE, EDINBURGH, 1892–3
Listed Category A

Three members of the Speculative Society (an Edinburgh public speaking and literary society dating from 1764), Edward Horsman, David Mure and James Moncrieff, founded Grange Cricket Club in 1832 on rough pasture belonging to Sir Thomas Dick Lauder at Grange House on the south side of Edinburgh. The first match was against the Brunswick Club, a wandering club,

formed mainly by staff and students of the University of Edinburgh in 1830. The club moved to another field at Grove Street in 1836, then to a pitch to the north of Fettes College in 1863, where a pavilion was constructed on the site of the current school pavilion. Finally, the club leased its current ground off Raeburn Place in 1871 and constructed a small brick pavilion. Edinburgh's Dean of Guild Court approved designs for a new pavilion by Cunningham, Blyth & Westland on 22 September 1892; Lord Moncrieff of Tulliebole opened the £1,400 pavilion the following year.

The game was ready to begin, the Cricketers were seen / With yellow shoes and jackets white, upon the Glasgow Green, / Leech, Wilkinson, and Currie too, and Southernden were there, / But though the day was fine, each face bore marks of dool and care.
The Chronicle had puffed the match, and from the town did pour / A motley mob of all degrees, – squire, commoner, and whore; / There was a smatch of all mankind, from saint down to the sinner, / Curdownie – Clelland, LL.D. – Stoddart – and Mr. Jenner.

'The Pump: ane righte lamentable dirge, composit be Bailzie Peacodde, poet Laureate to ye Cricket Club, rendered into modern verse by Dr. Minch', 1835[1]

Some historians argue that cricket evolved in medieval France, while others champion the Low Countries or the English Weald. Whatever the truth about its obscure origins, the modern game is widely regarded as a quintessentially English creation. Cricket is known to have been a school game in England since at least 1550, and an adult sport since 1611, when two players in Sussex were prosecuted for not observing the sabbath. Cricket flourished in England after the restoration of the monarchy in 1660, and appears to have spread to British colonies in North America, the West Indies and India by the early eighteenth century. Members of the Star and Garter Club first codified the Laws of Cricket in 1744 and modified them in 1774 to include lbw (leg before wicket), a middle stump and a maximum bat width. The Marylebone Cricket Club (MCC), founded in 1787, took on the custodianship of cricket's Code of Laws in 1788, and remains the worldwide authority to this day. In spite of its relatively small following in Scotland, cricket here has an interesting history and some attractive and unusual associated buildings.

The earliest appearance of the game in Scotland is not known, but it is thought likely that English troops serving in Scotland during and after the Jacobite Rising of 1745 practised the sport.

Café Royal, Edinburgh. Painted glass window
by Ballantine & Gardiner, about 1900
Photo: RCAHMS

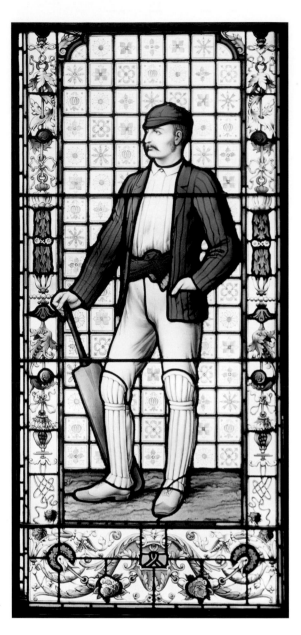

Certainly the game seems to have been played by soldiers in Perth in 1750, and a coterie of military and aristocratic Scots had become enthusiasts by the 1780s.[2] First among them was the cricket-mad Douglas Douglas-Hamilton, 8th Duke of Hamilton, who first spotted his bride-to-be, Elizabeth Burrell, wielding a cricket bat at the Oaks, Surrey, in 1777. It was reported that:

when she took the bat in hand, then her Diana-like air communicated an irresistible impression – She got more notches [runs, recorded by notches on a piece of wood] *in the first and second innings than any lady in the game, and at last bowled the Duke himself fairly out.*[3]

Visitors hoping to view Douglas-Hamilton's ducal home, Hamilton Palace, in 1781 found that 'as the Duke plays at cricket every afternoon, strangers don't get admittance'.[4] The Duke and his brother-in-law, Peter Burrell (later 1st Baron Gwydyr), were both members of the White Conduit Club of Islington, London, which had a very significant role in English cricket history, as its members were responsible for persuading Thomas Lord to establish what became Lord's Cricket Ground and for the foundation of the MCC in 1787. Lord, the son of Jacobite Scots whose lands were sequestered following the 1745 Rising, was the attendant and a bowler for the White Conduit Club. Fellow influential members included the Scots, Charles Lennox (later 4th Duke of Richmond and Lennox) and George Gordon (later 9th Marquess of Huntly).

The first recorded cricket match in Scotland is often stated as being between the Duke of Atholl's XI and Colonel George Talbot's XI at the 1st Earl of Cathcart's Schaw Park House, Alloa, on 3 September 1785 for an extravagant 1,000 guineas per side wager. Certainly it is recorded as a 'Grand Match' and the players' names and scores were reported in the *Caledonian Mercury* amongst other newspapers.[5] However, as the diary of the earl's daughter, Mary Graham (immortalised by Thomas Gainsborough's 'Beautiful Mrs Graham' portrait of 1775–7 in the National Gallery of Scotland), reveals, the grand match came at the end of a visit to Perthshire by Colonel Talbot and some fellow members of the White Conduit Club.[6] The White Conduit Club members, including Talbot himself and the Earl of Winchilsea, appear to have played in cricket matches at Blair Castle on 20 and 22 August 1785. Mary Graham's diary also records earlier matches between unidentified sides, possibly at her home, Balgowan House, on 21 July and 6 August 1785. Richard Alexander Oswald of Auchincruive in Ayrshire is credited with introducing cricket to the College Green in Glasgow when he arrived at the university in 1785.[7]

From these military and aristocratic beginnings in the late eighteenth century era of underarm bowling (overarm became legitimate in 1864), cricket developed a broader-based following in Scotland after the disruption of the Napoleonic

Manderston
Cricket Club
Pavilion, about
1900
Photo: Historic
Scotland,
Edinburgh

Wars in the first decade of the nineteenth century. Schools, such as the High School in Edinburgh, were playing cricket in the second decade of the nineteenth century, and the universities followed in the 1820s and 1830s. The cavalry stationed at Perth began playing on the North Inch in 1812. Informal games were also played in the 1820s at Bruntsfield Links in Edinburgh, where there were complaints about the disruption of the fairways by wickets, and at Glasgow Green, Arbroath and Glenpark, Greenock. Kelso Cricket Club, established in 1821, is the oldest continuously operating cricket club in Scotland, followed by Grange Cricket Club in Edinburgh established in 1832 and Clydesdale Cricket Club in Glasgow dating from 1848. The first three-day 'Grand Match' between William Clark's All England XI and a 'Twenty-two of Scotland' at the Grange Club's Grove Street ground in 1849 caused a sensation that set the game on a firm footing in Scotland.[8] Scotland played eleven-a-side from 1865. It is not known for certain when or where the first purpose-built cricket pavilion was constructed in Scotland, but there does seem to have been a pavilion at the second home of the Grange Club, Sparkes' Ground at Grove Park off Grove Street, Edinburgh, by 1849.[9] Other early pavilions included that of the Caledonian Cricket Club of Glasgow on their Burnbank ground (rebuilt by Queen's

Park Football Club at their first Hampden Park ground in 1878) and the one built by the Edinburgh Academicals to serve both the cricket and rugby teams at Raeburn Place in 1859. The Accies' £150 pavilion was described as 'an elegant and commodious structure' with a central dining room and rooms on either side, and was used as accommodation for the players and shelter from the wet for players and spectators alike.[10] The 'dining room' is more likely to have served as a venue for the great cricketing ritual of 'tea'.

Apart from a keen educational, military and aristocratic following, cricket also flourished where communities of immigrant English workers gathered, such as the Yorkshire, Lancashire and Leicestershire textile workers who came to the Borders towns of Hawick and Selkirk in the 1840s and 1850s.[11] By the 1870s, many mining and other industrial villages had their own teams. Often cricket clubs held annual games, races or sports days, from which amateur athletics emerged. Cricket was not confined to the Lowlands. In the 1850s there were cricket clubs in Fortrose, Cromarty, Inverness, Nairn and Tain amongst other Highland burghs. By the 1860s cricket was a significant sport in Glasgow. David Bone in his *Scottish Football Reminiscences and Sketches* of 1890 describes how the march of development

↘ BARRIE PAVILION, HILL OF KIRRIEMUIR, 1929
Listed Category B

The cricket enthusiast and author of *Peter Pan*, J.M. Barrie, gifted a £2,500 pavilion and camera obscura to his native town of Kirriemuir in 1929. The initial intention was to mark the scene of Barrie's childhood cricket games with a modest sports pavilion, but Barrie asked the architect, Frank D. Thomson of Dundee, to include something that children could also enjoy. Thomson, a keen photographer, suggested a camera obscura, an optical device that projects live images onto a screen in a darkened room by using mirrors. The camera obscura was duly incorporated into the roof of the entrance tower to provide panoramic views of the surrounding Angus countryside. Inside were a hall, dressing rooms and other accommodation 'of an up-to-date principle'. Barrie opened the unusual combination building on 7 June 1930 after being granted the freedom of the town.

in the city destroyed many of the old level cricket grounds, and association football took hold as a sport that could be played on smaller, rougher ground in all weathers and at less expense.[12] Many early association and rugby football clubs developed out of existing cricket clubs, and initially shared their grounds and pavilions. However, the smooth wickets required for cricket were difficult to achieve with winter games on the same field, so unless grounds were large enough to support various sports, separate cricket grounds became more usual. Cricket spread steadily throughout the country from the 1850s to the 1880s. In March 1893 the Cameron Highlanders, Dingwall, Elgin, Forres St Lawrence, Inverness College, Inverness Mechanics, Northern Counties, Nairn County and St Duthus (Tain) cricket clubs agreed to form the North of Scotland Cricket Association. In most cases clubs rented their grounds, but some enthusiastic landowners, for example the sports-loving Arthur Fitzgerald Kinnaird, 11th Lord Kinnaird of Rossie Priory, and Sir James Miller of Manderston, created their own grounds and pavilions. The Scottish Cricket Union (Cricket Scotland since 2001) was formed in 1908 as the governing body for the sport in Scotland. Although cricket had a secure, but not fanatical, following in Scotland throughout the twentieth century, it was not until 1994 that Scotland was elected to Associate Membership of the International Cricket Council (Icc) and took part in the Icc World Cup in 1997.

↘ POWERLEAGUE PAISLEY, BLACKHALL STREET, PAISLEY, RENFREWSHIRE, 1924–5
Listed Category B
Photo: Historic Scotland, Edinburgh

Built in 1924–5 as the Anchor Recreation Club for the workers of Anchor Mills, the large clubhouse was designed to face two separate sports grounds catering for cricket, bowling, putting and tennis. The local architects were Thomas Graham Abercrombie and James Steel Maitland.

GANNOCHY TRUST CRICKET PAVILION, DOOCOT PARK, KINCARRATHIE, PERTH, 1925
Listed Category B

Arthur Kinmond 'AK' Bell, of the Perth whisky company Arthur Bell & Sons, played for the Wolfhill, Perthshire and Grange Cricket Clubs and was president of the Scottish Cricket Union in 1912. He was a friend of the star Australian batsman, Don Bradman. AK's love of cricket led him to establish a fine cricket ground and pavilion in the grounds of his home, Kincarrathie House, in 1927. The pavilion and grounds were gifted to the Gannochy Trust, established in 1937 to continue AK's philanthropic interests. Smart, Stewart & Mitchell's quirky design for the Doocot Park Pavilion includes an octagonal club-room and balcony. The larch-clad building is so rustic in character that it is often described as the 'tree house'. It opened on 25 April 1925 with a match between the local Jeanfield and Balhousie teams.

Curling

THOMSON'S TOWER, DUDDINGSTON LOCH, EDINBURGH, 1825

Listed Category B

Although curling had long been practised at Duddingston Loch, and a local club had existed there from the middle of the eighteenth century, it was not until the Duddingston Curling Society was formally reconstituted on 17 January 1795 that the sport began to flourish. The annual freeze attracted Edinburgh's aristocracy, gentry and eminent professionals to Duddingston Loch. Many were appointed to honorary positions in the society: chaplain; officer, Master of Stones; surgeon; poet-laureate, medallist; and counsellors. Thanks to the enthusiastic support of the local minister, Revd William Bennet, the society built a small oval curling house, or 'hall', adjacent to the loch on the glebe lands of Duddingston Kirk. This was replaced in 1825 by the current octagonal tower, designed by William Henry Playfair, which comprised two unconnected rooms: the lower was designed to store the members' curling stones and equipment; the upper room was intended as a members' meeting room.

In the winter season, curling and skating are very common amusements. During hard frost, some of our lochs present a very gay and animating appearance. The skater performs his evolutions, the stone thunders along the ice amid the cheers of the spectators, the graceful forms of the fair move up and down on the slippery promenade, giving additional interest to the scene. Curling levels all distinctions, the laird and the labourer, the master and the servant, the clergyman and the clown, are all on an equality at this game.

New Statistical Account, 1839[1]

Known as the 'Roarin' Game' after the sound of the stones on the ice, curling's origins are disputed, with some arguing that it was brought to Scotland from the Low Countries, and others putting the case for a Scottish origin. The Little Ice Age, which lasted from the mid-sixteenth century to the late nineteenth century, brought reasonably reliable freezing conditions in winter to enable lochs, ponds, rivers and canals to serve as sheets (playing surfaces) for curling. The game was probably being played in Scotland from at least the early part of the sixteenth century, as suggested by a stone that is dated 1511, which was discovered near Stirling.[2] The 1685 inventory of General Tam Dalyell's House of the Binns, shows that early curling 'stones' were also made of lead and iron, and even wood.[3] Henry Adamson's poem of 1620, *The Muse's Threnodie,* provides the first written reference to the term 'curling'.[4] A curling society existed at Kinross from at least 1667, but it was re-established in 1818.[5] Kilsyth Curling Club, which was constituted in 1716, is thought to be the oldest continuously operating curling club in the world. Most early curling took place at pre-existing water features, but certainly by the beginning of the eighteenth century, ponds were being created specifically for curling. John Cramichael, 3rd Earl of Hyndford, created a large formal landscape at Carmichael House in Lanarkshire in the 1730s, the central feature of which was a long rectangular 'canal', known from the outset as 'the curling pond'.[6] The compilers of

The small stone-built curling house on the edge of Lindores Loch was constructed in 1871 for the Abdie Curling Club. Originally thatched with reeds from the loch, the hut is now roofed with corrugated iron. The simple interior remains much as built, with a small fireplace, shelves for storing the curling stones, a table and benches.

the 1828 *Kilmarnock Treatise on Curling* characterised curling as a Lowland sport, practised mainly in parts of Lanarkshire, Peeblesshire, Midlothian, Perthshire, Dumfriesshire and Ayrshire. John Kerr's 1890 history of the sport identifies at least forty-two societies in existence by 1800, the most northerly at Forfar, and the most southerly at Sanquhar.[7]

With the advent of hollow-ground stones in 1784, regular circular stones replaced the old river and boulder stones, and a greater consistency of rules, field of play and equipment began to emerge between different clubs and venues. Famously curling was played by all ranks of society, but in rural areas it was particularly popular with farmers, masons and others whose work was disrupted by hard frost and freezing temperatures. Most clubs required their members to provide themselves with two stones, and kept a supply of club-owned stones for general use. With the advent of the new, more expensive, circular stones came an increasing need for secure storage facilities. At Blairgowrie the stones were kept outdoors, chained together beside the curling pond, until a stone-built curling house was erected for £7 in 1819.[8] Many societies arranged for cartage from town centres. A minute of the Duddingston Curling Society of February 1795 describes 'the reduced situation of their curling-stones, owing to their being left in a destitute state in the open field'. The same meeting resolved to build the society's first curling hut in the glebe adjoining Duddingston Loch.[9]

Edinburgh's legal elite formed a large part of the membership of the Duddingston Curling Society, so it is perhaps no surprise that the first 'Code of Curling Laws' was drawn up by a special committee of that society in 1803 and adopted in 1806. These rules were widely taken up by other societies, and form the basis of the modern game. Other clubs also began to make provision for the permanent storage of stones and equipment. In 1804 the Dunfermline Curling Club authorised the reconstruction of the stair on the south side of the pond so that the stones, crampets (iron plates for standing on the ice) and brooms could be stored underneath. Unlike many other sports that were disrupted by the Napoleonic Wars in the early years of the nineteenth century, curling seems to have thrived. By 1838 there were almost 200 clubs, mainly concentrated in Ayrshire, Dumfriesshire, Midlothian, Fife, Lanarkshire, Perthshire, Renfrewshire and Stirlingshire. One of the reasons for the substantial increase in clubs was the invention in 1813 of shallow, level, artificial ponds by the retired surgeon and obsessive curler, John Cairnie of Curling Hall, Largs.[10] Artificial ponds had been created previously by damming of burns, but the water often varied in depth and could take some time to freeze. Cairnie's shallow artificial ponds, created from either macadamised puddle clay or flat paving stones jointed with mastic cement, allowed the formation of a safe and level curling rink in just one night of freezing temperatures. Another accompanying development, which made the curling huts into more social spaces, was the provision of fireplaces for warming players, making hot drinks and heating stew. Artificial ponds of the late nineteenth century were made of concrete and sometimes lit by electric lights.[11]

John Cairnie was also to become the first president of the Grand Caledonian Curling Club on 25 July 1838. Known as the Royal Caledonian Curling Club from 1843, and managed by representative members of local clubs, its purpose was, and remains, as a national governing body for the sport. Another important function of the Royal Caledonian Curling Club was to promote the sport, which it did by providing medals for competitions between member clubs, establishing 'provinces' of clubs to enable larger 'bonspiels' (tournaments), publishing its *Annual*, and by inaugurating Grand Matches between the north and south of Scotland. Such was the success of promoting the sport that almost every mainland parish had a curling pond, and over 2,300 sites are recorded as having been used for curling at one time or another from Wigtownshire to Shetland.[12]

Curling was so popular in the 1830s that numerous attempts were made to create summer rinks of plate iron or timber. *The New Statistical Account* of 1833 noted:

Gosford Curling House, Gosford House,
early nineteenth century
Listed Category B

Banchory Curling Club Hut, Burnett Park,
Banchory, 1887

Easter Balmoral Curling Pavilion,
about 1905
Listed Category C

*Among the usual games of the country, that of
curling has lately afforded considerable amusement
as a summer exercise, being practised with wooden
blocks, shaped like a curling stone, on a rink of
the ordinary length made of deal, smoothed, and
rendered slippery with soap. To diminish the friction,
the block is made to slide, not on its entire base, but
on three nobs, equidistant, projecting a few lines,
and well rounded. Judging by the hard hits, the glee
of the players, with their vociferations of censure or
applause, as remarkable in this as in winter curling,
it would seem that the artificial method is nowise
inferior, except in the fitness of scenery, and the
effect of wonted associations.*[13]

Indoor curling was boosted by the construction
of parish halls in the second half of the nineteenth
century, where 'summer ice', a miniature curling
game using iron 'stones' on highly polished floors
became popular.[14]

From twenty-eight affiliated clubs with 893
members in 1838, the Royal Caledonian Curling
Club prospered to 465 affiliated clubs and 18,647
members in 1888. Many clubs were not affiliated to
the Royal Caledonian Curling Club, and these too
flourished into the late nineteenth century. The vast
majority of rinks were on artificial ponds, many of
which were created on private estates of the gentry
and aristocracy. Although women played the sport
from at least the second decade of the nineteenth
century, it was not until 1895 that two ladies' clubs,
Hercules Ladies' Curling Club (Elie, Fife) and
Boghead Ladies' Curling Club (Bathgate, West
Lothian) were admitted to the Royal Club. The first
two-room, joint ladies' and men's, curling house
was opened at Elie on 12 October 1899 as noted in
the Royal Caledonian Club's *Annual 1899–1900*:

*The house is in two divisions, one for each club.
The gentlemen's house… is fitted up with tables,
chairs, and an excellent stove, the gift of Captain
Scott-Davidson, while the curling stones are ingen-
iously boxed in what serves as a seat all round the
house. The ladies' house…is provided with cloakroom and lavatory, and is handsomely furnished
with cushioned seats and curtains, while the stones*

PARTICK CURLING CLUB PAVILION, VICTORIA PARK, GLASGOW, 1900
Listed Category C

Partick Curling Club gained a twenty-year lease of ground at the west end of the newly-formed Victoria (then Whiteinch) Park in 1893 and soon built a curling pond there. The railway and public works contractor William Kennedy presented a new curling house in 1900, and his business partners M. Hunter Kennedy and John G Kennedy added two artificial rinks (lit by electric lamps) in 1902. The red brick 'house' is a handsome miniature Glasgow Style pavilion with deep overhanging eaves and dumpy red sandstone columns. The pavilion contains three rooms: a club room, heated by an open fire on the west side; a toilet; and a locker room, which still contains the original wooden lockers used for storing the members' stones.

are placed under the seats as in the gentlemen's house. Here also there is a large, handsome stove, the gift of General Morgan, Elie.

Not all ponds had curling huts or houses for storage of stones and equipment, but some land-owners provided huts and ponds on condition that they were maintained by the local club, and in other cases local clubs built their own huts and ponds by subscription. Many curling huts were little more than basic utilitarian timber sheds, but others were larger and more elaborate, built of corrugated-iron sheeting over a timber frame, or in stone or brick. Huts on country estates often took the form of rustic, picturesque 'fog houses' (ornamental summerhouses), with decorative applied timber-work of tree-trunks and branches, such as the one at Gordon Castle, Fochabers, or rockwork or boulder construction, like the curling hut at Gosford House, Aberlady. Huts near natural ponds or lochs were frequently thatched with local reeds. By their nature, curling huts were usually remote from everyday oversight, so needed to be secured with shutters or iron bars over the windows. Internally the huts were lined with either open shelves or boxes for pairs of curling stones, and some had a fireplace or stove for warming the curlers and benches for changing shoes. At the grander end of the scale, the curling house designed by Robert Weir Schultz for the Marquess of Bute at Falkland Palace in 1896 had two rooms: one for the Falkland Curling Club members; the other for the Marquess and his family, who had rights to curl at any time.

From the end of the Little Ice Age in the last years of the nineteenth century, and the construction of the Crossmyloof Ice Rink, Glasgow, by the Scottish Ice Rink Company in 1907, regular outdoor curling began to decline and the most active clubs adapted to reliable indoor conditions all year round. Further information on the later history of indoor rinks can be found in the section on ice skating.

Football

**GALA FAIRYDEAN FOOTBALL CLUB STAND,
NETHER ROAD, GALASHIELS, 1963–4**
Listed Category A
Photo: RCAHMS

Gala Fairydean Football Club moved to their current
ground at Nether Road in 1962, taking over the site
from the Galashiels Rovers Rugby Club. It was another
two years before the club managed to raise by means
of a public lottery the necessary £25,000 for a 620-seat
replacement stand. The designer of this extraordinarily
sculptural structure was the Yorkshire architect Peter
Womersley, who for most of his career lived at Gattonside
near Melrose. Ove Arup & Partners provided engineering
expertise. The stand is constructed from air-entrained
poured concrete. The whole geometric design is based
on angles of thirty and sixty degrees and on five-inch
modules, representing the width of the Douglas fir boards
of the formwork into which the concrete was poured.

**Brissit brawnis and brokin banis,
Stride, discord and waistie wanis.
Crukit in eild syne halt withal,
Thir are the bewties of the fute-ball
[Bruises and broken bones, strife, discord and
futile blows, crooked and lame in old age, these are
the beauties of the football]**

Anonymous late sixteenth-century poem, 'The
Bewties of the Fute-Ball' from the Richard Maitland
manuscripts in the Pepys Library of Magdalene
College, Cambridge

Like archery, golf, curling, bowling and royal tennis,
'the beautiful game' has ancient roots in Scotland,
dating back in different forms for at least 600
years. Much of the historic stadium and stand
architecture associated with modern association
football developed between the end of the nineteenth century and the mid-twentieth century, but
little now survives. Numerous stadium disasters
around the world, including the 1971 Ibrox tragedy
and the Hillsborough disaster of 1989, have led to
the re-design or replacement of most large-scale
venues to all-seater spectator stands in Scotland in
the last twenty years.

 An Act of the Scottish Parliament of 26 May
1424 decreed that 'it is statut and the king forbiddis
that ony man play at the futball undir the pain of iiij
d.'[it is decreed and the king forbids that any man
play football, punishable by a fine of 4 pence].[1] The
ban was repeated in later years, along with golf, to
ensure that there was no distraction from learning
the military skill of archery. In spite of the various
bans, a courtly version of the game appears to have
flourished in the yards and grounds adjacent to
palaces such as Stirling and Edzell. The Lord High
Treasurer's accounts show that James IV paid two
shillings for a bag of 'fut ballis' on 11 April 1497.[2]
The world's oldest football, thought to date from
the 1540s, was discovered in the rafters behind
the ceiling of the Queen's Chamber at Stirling
Castle. As the rules were not codified, it is difficult
to be certain of the nature of the medieval game.
Documentary evidence suggests that at least some

GALA FAIRYDEAN FOOTBALL CLUB STAND, NETHER ROAD, GALASHIELS, 1963–4
Listed Category A

The bank of seating forms an apparently solid triangular wedge over the ground floor changing rooms, showers, clubroom facilities and kitchen. Four tapering triangular piers support the cantilevered canopy, which is also wedge-shaped. The pitch floodlights were built into the underside of the canopy. Sheets of safety glass protect the ends of the stand and a screen wall of glazing and black brick panels extends along the full length of the ground floor facilities. On either side of the stand are external staircases and adjoining 'concrete umbrellas' that shelter the turnstiles. As completed in 1965, the building was intended to be capable of extension in further modules if necessary. Stylistically the stand is 'Brutalist', a descriptive term applied to monumental buildings of *béton brut*, or raw concrete, frequently where the texture of the timber formwork on the poured concrete, the structural framework and the various functions of different parts of the building are all clearly visible.

games were played over relatively small-scale areas, between ten and twenty players took part, and kicking, goal-keeping and 'making' goals were involved.[3] Certainly numerous reports indicate that competition could be ferocious.

'Ba games' that still take place at Duns, Jedburgh, Roxburgh, Kirkwall and Scone are thought to be variants on medieval football, where a 'ba', or ball, is manhandled to one or other end of the town by large teams of 'uppies' and 'doonies'. John Stark's *Picture of Edinburgh* published in 1806 described the state of football as 'also decayed in Edinburgh, though in the country parts of Scotland this amusement is still kept up'.[4] The married and unmarried women of Musselburgh played an annual football match on Shrove Tuesday, which was usually won by the married women.[5] John Hope, a seventeen-year old trainee Edinburgh lawyer, established the earliest known 'Foot-ball club' in the world in 1824 (revived 2007). A letter of 1825 in the National Records of Scotland refers to a game involving thirty-nine players and sticks as goals, and 'such kicking of shins and such tumbling'.[6] The only surviving rules of Hope's club prohibited tripping, but allowed pushing and holding and the lifting of the pig's bladder ball.[7] A 'chairman' seems to have acted as a referee. The University of Glasgow historian David Murray recalled football on the College Green in 1865 as 'a rough and tumble game in which the contending sides swept across the low green from Blackfriars Street to the New Vennel and back again like the hordes of Attila, with no goal posts, uneven team numbers of up to 100 players per side, no distinguishing kit for each team, and no limit to the size of the pitch'.[8]

The start of the modern game of soccer can be dated to the formation of the Football Association by eleven London clubs and schools on 26 October 1863, and the subsequent approval of the thirteen 'Laws of the Game' on 8 December 1863. Queen's Park Football Club in Glasgow was the first Scottish club to form for the purpose of playing association football in 1867, and the first match was played against the Thistle Football Club in the South Side Park on 1 August of the following year.[9] On 30 November 1872 the first official international football match between Scotland and England took place at the West of Scotland Cricket Ground, Hamilton Crescent, Partick with 4,000 spectators watching the nil-nil draw. The Scottish Football Association formed from eight clubs (Queen's Park, Clydesdale, Vale of Leven, Dumbreck, Third Lanark, Eastern, Granville and Kilmarnock) was established on 13 March 1873 and adopted the rules of the Football Association in London.[10] The first season saw Queen's Park defeat Clydesdale to win the Scottish Association Challenge Cup on Saturday 21 March 1874 in front of several thousand spectators at the first Hampden Park ground. The cup was made by George Edward & Sons of Glasgow, and is now recognised as the oldest trophy in association football anywhere in the world. The *Dundee Courier*'s report of the match noted: 'We may add that in the short space of four years football has become a most popular game in Scotland, clubs rising up everywhere.'[11] Such was the astonishing success of the game that by 1880 over a 1,000 senior and junior clubs had formed throughout Scotland.[12] The Scottish Football League dates from 1890 with professional football following shortly afterwards in 1893.

Queen's Park Football Club was one of the most successful of the early clubs in Scotland, credited with founding the 'passing game'. Initially the club played on the recreation ground at Queen's Park on the south side of Glasgow, but there were no facilities for either players or their rapidly growing number of supporters on the communal playing fields there.[13] The balls, goal posts, ropes, flags and other equipment were stored in the lodge to the nearby 'Deaf & Dumb Institution'. On 20 October 1873 the club took the momentous decision to rent their own ground across the Cathcart Road at Hampden Park from the town council. The park was named after the neighbouring Hampden Terrace, which in turn was named by the builder George Eadie after John Hampden, one of the Parliamentarians who sparked the English Civil War in 1642. The team

adopted a 'uniform' of red cap, black and white inch stripe jersey and stockings, and white knickerbockers for the first match at Hampden Park. A dedicated playing area enabled the club to fence off their ground and take the innovative steps of charging an entrance fee for individual matches and selling season tickets. The admission fees and members' subscriptions provided a substantial and reliable income, which the club invested in facilities. The first association football-related building in Scotland was a modest wooden clubhouse, commissioned for £21 from a Mr Nicol, presumably John Nicol, who is recorded as a slater, bricklayer and plasterer in the Glasgow Post Office Directory of 1874–5.[14] Next came a utilitarian grandstand, eighty yards long and six seats deep, built by J. & J. Phillips, wrights and builders, for £238 in 1876.[15] Two years later the *Dundee Courier* and other newspapers reported on the club's largely successful experiment with Siemens electric floodlights, hosting an evening charity match between Third Lanark (three goals) and Rangers (two goals) in front of some 20,000 spectators on 4 November 1878.[16] At about this time the club purchased the redundant pavilion of the Caledonian Cricket Club and transported it from Burnbank in the West End of the city. The Queen's Park club subsequently moved grounds on two occasions, with later developments leaving no trace of the original historic structures at the first Hampden Park.

The sixpence ground admission charge set by Queen's Park was highly influential for the other association clubs, who also sought to maximise their income by acquiring and enclosing their own grounds and attracting paying spectators.[17] Apart from making special transport arrangements to encourage attendance, most clubs constructed 'viewing slopes' of cinder and gravel banks and also covered stands, for which spectators paid an additional fee (retained by the home club – the ground entry charges were shared between the competing clubs). The total enclosure of the pitch by stands and terraces prevented non-paying spectators from viewing the field of play. There were reduced charges for children, and women and uniformed servicemen were admitted without charge until 1918. The construction of the Cathcart Railway in 1883 caused the removal of the Queen's Park club from the first Hampden to a second Hampden just to the east (now Cathkin Park). Although only the viewing slopes, some crush barriers, the track and pitch now survive, it was also a site of pioneering football architecture in Scotland. Glasgow architect and club member, John Hamilton, was responsible for the layout of the oval stadium and the design of the country's first brick football pavilion, which incorporated the decorative bargeboards of the old Caledonian Cricket Club pavilion and contained changing rooms and a committee room.[18] A grandstand lined the south side of the pitch, and sculpted

SOUTH STAND, IBROX FOOTBALL STADIUM, GLASGOW, 1923–9
Listed Category B

In 1887 Fred Braby & Co., 'contractors for pavilions, stands, barricades and requisites for football and cricket enclosures', built the first Ibrox Park with a single wooden stand and terraces laid out in an oval around a running track. A separate single storey timber and corrugated-iron pavilion housed the players and officials. Ibrox Park proved popular with the rapidly increasing population of Govan, many of which worked in the shipyards and engineering works. In 1892, one of the stands partially collapsed under the pressure of the 21,000 crowd attending the Scotland-England international. The capacity constraints, the end of the existing lease in 1899 and competition from rival venues at Celtic Park and the proposed third Hampden prompted Rangers to form a limited company to raise funds to lease a new adjacent site and to rebuild Ibrox from scratch. On 14 July 1899 Leitch & Davies, consulting engineers and factory architects, submitted plans to Govan's Dean of Guild Court for a new stand at the extended Ibrox ground. Archibald Leitch's new plan proposed moving the pitch 150 yards west to its current location. Driven by the relatively short term (ten years) of the new lease, much of the second Ibrox comprised steel and timber stands that were intended to be capable of disassembly and re-use on another site. The separate pavilion incorporated seating under the verandas for 1,715 people, dressing rooms, a boardroom, manager's room and gymnasium. The north stand re-used the roof of the old stand, and Leitch designed a new south stand with a rooftop telegraph and press box. The pitch was surrounded by a cinder running track.

As a consequence of the partial collapse of the timber terracing in 1902, and also the club's purchase of the ground in 1904, which allowed long-term planning, Leitch redesigned the terraces to earthen embankments with concrete steps, eventually increasing capacity to about 83,000 by the early 1920s. The huge success of the club under the management of Bill Struth from 1920 led to the commission of the largest and most expensive grand-stand in Leitch's career, the new south stand of 1923–9. The opening programme described the 'epic features' of the lavish £95,000 administrative offices and stand, which included 1,123 tons of steel, over a million Welsh bricks, 10,000 yds of timber flooring, 6,000 yds of patent 'Kleine' fire-resistant flooring, 10,000 tip-up seats, two miles of electric cabling, 11,600 feet of steel windows, forty-four Ellison turnstiles, 2,450 yds of plastering, 2,000 feet of mahogany panelling, 3,000 feet oak panelling, 3,000 feet Port Orford Cedar, 370 yds of Terazzo flooring and 1,850 ft² of marble and tile work. For the first time at Ibrox, there was no separate pavilion and the accommodation for the players and administration was integrated into the main stand. In many ways the imposing street elevation and lavish interiors of the stand reflected the grandiose boardroom blocks fronting the engineering sheds of Glasgow's many factories, shipyards and works, such as the Fairfield Shipyard and Engine Works in nearby Govan Road. Although the south stand, now known as the Bill Struth Stand, was almost completely rebuilt and extended upwards by architect Gareth Hutchinson and engineers Blyth & Blyth in 1990–4, the great red-brick south frontage remains and many of the fine administrative interiors survive including the main stair, the Blue Room, the Trophy Room, the manager's office and the dressing rooms.

earthen viewing slopes enclosed the other sides of the great amphitheatre, with a separate players' and officials' pavilion at the south-west corner. A cinder running and cycling track surrounded the pitch and two tennis courts were incorporated at the east end, primarily as training facilities for the players, but also for more general sports days. Architects Ninian Macwhannel and John Rogerson enlarged the pavilion in 1889 to accommodate more recreational, social and training facilities for members including a 37.5 feet by 16 feet gymnasium, separate shower bathrooms for each team, a reading and games room, and an enlarged committee room. John Bennie Wilson designed roofs for the previously uncovered stands in 1889, the first press box for twenty reporters and a telegraph office were opened in October 1891, numerous 'pay boxes' were added at the entrance to the ground before 1892, and four state-of-the-art turnstiles were installed in December 1894.[19] Many extraordinary matches were played at the ground, including the game between Renton and West Bromwich Albion on 19 May 1888, when the West Dunbartonshire village became the first 'Champions of the United Kingdom and the World'.[20]

Although Queen's Park led the way in the development of both the game and the construction of facilities, many other clubs began to lay out their grounds and build pavilions, stands and viewing slopes in the 1870s and 1880s including: Kilmarnock at the first Rugby Park (1877); Dundee United at Tannadice Park (1883); Dunfermline Athletic at East End Park (1885); Heart of Midlothian at Tynecastle in Edinburgh (1886); Clachnacuddin at Grant Street Park in Inverness (1886); Rangers at the first Ibrox Park (1887); Montrose at Links Park (1887); Celtic at the first Celtic Park in Glasgow (1888); Ayr United at Somerset Park (1888) and Forfar Athletic at Station Park (1888). Many grounds were shared with other sports, such as cricket, rugby, athletics and cycling.

With the continuing success of association football, the larger clubs all looked to expand on new sites in the 1890s. Brother Walfrid of the Catholic institute of Marist Brothers had formed Celtic Football Club in November 1877 to alleviate poverty in the East End of Glasgow by raising money for his charity, the Poor Children's Dinner Table. The phenomenal success of the club and an increase in rent for the first Celtic Park to the north-east

of junction of Springfield Road and London Road prompted a move to the current 'Paradise' site next to the Janefield Cemetery, or Eastern Necropolis, to the north-west of the same junction. The new 57,000-capacity ground, described by the *Glasgow Herald* as 'second to none in Scotland', opened with an athletics and cycling meeting on 13 August 1892 attended by 14,000 spectators. A record-breaking 50,000 spectators witnessed the two-all draw between Scotland and England in April 1894, and one hundred journalists sent reports by telegraph and telephone from the extended press box.[21] Like the second Hampden, Celtic Park consisted of a separate two-storey storey rustic timber pavilion with a veranda, two grandstands set on the long sides of an oval track and playing area, and great banks of curved viewing mounds. The innovations here were the inclusion of two tracks: an inner cinder running track and an outer cycling track,

later upgraded to cement to host the World Cycling Championships in 1897. Timber terraces on steel columns set in concrete were added to some of the viewing mounds for this event. In 1899 the engineers Wylie and Black of St Vincent Street, Glasgow, designed the 'the biggest stand on earth or thereabouts', which was intended to attract new supporters, particularly women, by setting new standards of luxury and comfort as detailed in the *Dundee Courier*:

Fin-de-siecle football accommodation is coming to something, if one may believe all one hears. Celtic's new stand, which has been on hand since January last, and which, when finished, will cost nearly £6,600, is 70 yards long, 46 feet deep, and has seating accommodation for 2,000. The seats are tip-up chairs, upholstered in green leather. In front the stand is fitted with glass windows, which can be raised at will, and so make the structure

Celtic Park, Glasgow
Photo: RCAHMS

In 1887, a meeting convened by Marist monk Brother Walfrid to tackle the problems of social deprivation among the Irish immigrant community resulted in the formation of Celtic Football Club. Walfrid and a group of volunteers built the original Celtic Park in 1888. In 1892, after a huge increase in annual rent, another army of helpers was corralled to construct a replacement stadium across the street on the site of a disused Parkhead brickworks. Today the 60,506-capacity stadium – still standing on the 1892 site – is the largest football ground in Scotland.

Ibrox Stadium, Glasgow
Photo: RCAHMS

Formed in 1872 by a group of rowing enthusiasts, Rangers Football Club moved to Ibrox in 1887, taking up a pitch immediately to the east of the current stadium. The site of modern Ibrox was occupied from 1899 and the first notable development came in 1929 with the construction by celebrated stadium architect Archibald Leitch of the tall, renaissance red-brick stand on Edmiston Drive – with 10,000 seats, the largest and most lavish that had ever been built. Leitch's stand remains today as a Category B listed building incorporated into the modern redevelopment of Ibrox, now a 51,082-capacity all-seater stadium.

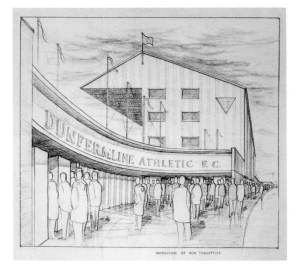

A sketch proposal for the entrance and turnstiles at Dunfermline Athletic's East End Park by Shearer & Annand, 1957
Photo: RCAHMS

entirely open. Access is gained by a covered entrance on London Road side of the field, and there is a transfer gate admitting from the inside of the reserved enclosure. It is expected that the various conveniences and new entrance, which will prevent all crushing, will bring a new set of followers to the game. At the end of the stand is a handsomely fitted-up lavatory, one for each sex. Above the stand, reached by a special stair, is the press box, and a telegraph instrument room, both of which are fitted up in the best styles. The stand is undoubtedly the finest in the kingdom, and marks an epoch in up-to-date arrangements.[22]

Although the Celtic experiment with a glazed stand was unsuccessful (it attracted condensation and was demolished in 1929), the design concerns for comfort, clear sightlines, crowd management and safety were to echo through the twentieth century. As the pioneering research of Simon Inglis has demonstrated, a new era in stadium design in the UK really began with the construction of stadia for Kilmarnock at Rugby Park and Rangers at Ibrox by the Glasgow consulting engineer, factory architect and Light Blues supporter, Archibald 'Archie' Leitch in 1899.[23] Leitch and his firm went on to design stands and stadia for some of the most famous clubs in English and Scottish football including Queen's Park, Celtic, Hearts, Dundee, Sheffield, Fulham, Arsenal, Manchester United, Chelsea, Everton, Liverpool, Tottenham, West Ham and Aston Villa. For the mostpart Leitch's designs were utilitarian, but they introduced a number of benefits for supporters including regular steps, measured risers, solid footings, fixed steel barriers, designated aisles and good sightlines to all parts of the ground. Leitch's estimates had a tendency to be far lower than the eventual building costs, but his structures of timber, steel, corrugated iron, and

later concrete, were still relatively cheap and quick to construct.

By the time of its completion in April 1900, the second Ibrox Park, with a capacity of 79,877, was the largest purpose-built football stadium in the world. The capacity was only tested at the first professional international between Scotland and England on 5 April 1902, during which part of the wooden south-west terrace collapsed, killing twenty-five people and injuring more than 500.[24] The causes of the disaster were disputed between the designer and the contractor, but the devastated Leitch was determined to continue in practice, putting the lessons of Ibrox to good purpose in ensuring as far as possible the safety of future stadium designs. There continued to be no statutory regulation of large public venues until the second Ibrox disaster in 1971 when sixty-six people were killed and over 600 were injured prompted the Safety of Sports Grounds Act of 1975. Before that date many of the large football clubs were regarded as insatiable in their greed for paying spectators, often at the expense of safety. After 1902 Leitch used a system of earth embankments with regular stepped terraces of timber (in-situ concrete from 1908), distributing passages, crush rails, sunken aisles and continuous barriers. Leitch even patented his own distinctive crush barrier in 1906. In many cases Leitch's terraces were sunk a little below the level of the pitch to maximise spectator numbers, reduce the required rake, lower construction costs and improve drainage. Typical features of later Leitch stadia of the 1920s were a gable over the centre of the stand and the use of two tiers of stand seating with steel lattice balustrades along the upper tier.

Spurred on by the construction of the huge stadia at Celtic Park and Ibrox Park, and also by the end of the lease at the second Hampden, Queen's Park purchased 12.5 acres of farmland at Mount Florida in 1900. The engineer, surveyor, cyclist and Queen's Park member, Alexander Blair, laid out a huge oval enclosure of embanked terraces with lateral and radial aisles, while the prominent

Ibrox Stadium,
interior view of
first floor staircase
Photo: RCAHMS

Glasgow architect James Miller was selected to design the two 2,200-seater south grandstands and central pavilion. Although Miller's 1902 designs for the pavilion echoed his exotic towers at the 1901 Glasgow International Exhibition, the club struggled with the expense of the 57,000 capacity ground and eventually settled for a simpler linking stand with a press box above and player and club accommodation below designed by Babtie, Shaw & Morton, engineers, in 1914.[25] The enormous, but still only partially complete, third Hampden Park opened on 31 October 1903 with a game between Queen's Park and Celtic. The worst rioting yet witnessed at a football ground occurred in 1909 between Celtic and Rangers fans, resulting in the destruction of the turnstile block. By 1905 the extension of the terraces had increased the capacity of the ground to 80,000, and by 1910 it was 120,000. Hampden was the largest purpose-built stadium in the world, and was to remain so until the opening of the Maracanã Stadium in Rio de Janeiro, Brazil, in 1950.[26] Between 1927 and 1937 Archibald Leitch's firm extended the south stand, installed his patent crush barriers and rebuilt the north stand with its distinctive projecting towers. This was the period when the stadium acquired the famous Hampden Roar, first noticed during a Scotland-England match in 1929, when the injured Alex Jackson could hear the crowd responding to his team-mate Alec Cheyne's last minute equaliser from a mile away at the Victoria Infirmary. The 1937 Scotland-England match attracted an official record attendance of 149,415 spectators, but up to 20,000 additional people are thought to have entered the ground without tickets. Apart from its oval arrangement, little now remains of Leitch's Hampden, which was redeveloped in the 1990s.

Leitch's stadium legacy continued to exert a conservative architectural influence over the design and modification of stadia and stands in Scotland during the mid – twentieth century. It was not until the 1960s that the influence of Modernist architecture was felt, and then on a modest scale, such as the small masterpieces at Dam Park, Ayr and Gala Fairydean in Galashiels, where the concrete structures are revealed in sculptural form.

Golf

ROYAL BURGESS GOLFING SOCIETY CLUBHOUSE, WHITEHOUSE ROAD, EDINBURGH, 1896–7
Listed Category B
Photo: Royal Burgess Golfing Society

The Royal Burgess Golfing Society is generally acknowledged as the oldest golf club with a continuous history in the world. The Society began its existence as the Edinburgh Burgess Golfing Society at Bruntsfield Links, Edinburgh, in about 1735. As Bruntsfield became overcrowded, the Society moved to Musselburgh golf course in 1874, then finally to their own course at Barnton, which they purchased from the Maitland family in 1894. On 11 May 1897 the former Prime Minister, Lord Rosebery, opened the new clubhouse, designed by the architect and keen amateur golfer Robert Macfarlane Cameron, and described by the *Edinburgh Evening News* as 'the finest and at the same time most complete, establishment of any golf club in the country'.

Of this diversion the Scots are so fond that, when the weather will permit, you may see a multitude of all ranks, from the senator of justice to the lowest tradesmen, mingled together in their shirts, and following the balls with the utmost eagerness.

Tobias Smollett, *The Expedition of Humphrey Clinker*, London, 1771, p.236

The origins of golf are obscure and hotly disputed, with claims for its invention in countries as far afield as the Netherland, France and China dating back to the 10th century. What is clear, however, is that the principal ingredients of the modern game came together in Scotland by the middle of the eighteenth century. Accompanying the development and refinement of the sport in the second half of the nineteenth century, architects sought to give form to a new building type, the clubhouse or 'nineteenth hole' – a mixture of a convivial gentlemen's club and a functional space for changing clothes and storing equipment.

The earliest 'golf' in Scotland seems to have taken several forms, depending on the social class. An Act of the Scottish Parliament of 6 March 1458 decreed that 'the futbawe ande the golf be utirly criyt doune and nocht wsyt' [football and golf should be completely condemned and stopped], apparently in an attempt to promote archery and other more useful military skills, and to put a stop to the dangerous hockey-like game that occupied the public spaces and kirkyards of several towns.[1] At the other end of the social scale, royalty and the nobility seem to have adopted two further forms of genteel 'golf': a short game with soft balls and shinty sticks; and a long game with specialist equipment made by artisans. The Lord High Treasurer's accounts of 21 September 1502 record the purchase of equipment for James IV: *Item the xxi day of September to the bower (bowmaker) of Sanct Johnstoun (Perth) for clubbes xiiij (14) shillings*.[2] Other sixteenth – and seventeenth-century accounts for the purchase of equipment show not just that royalty and nobility enjoyed the long game, but that increasingly it was taken up by the

GOLFERS' BRIDGE OVER THE SWILKEN BURN AND CLUBHOUSE, OLD COURSE, ST ANDREWS,
Listed Category B

Although probably built for drovers and their stock, and subsequently much reconstructed, this little hump-backed bridge dates back to at least the eighteenth century as the 'Goffers' Bridge', or Golfers' Bridge. More recently it has appropriated the name 'Swilken Bridge' from the old road bridge that stood to its south. Straddling the Swilken Burn between the 1st and 18th fairways of the Old Course, the Golfers' Bridge is now one of the most famous structures in any sport. John Henry Taylor, James Braid, Bobby Jones, Sam Snead, Bobby Locke, Peter Thomson, Jack Niklaus, Seve Ballesteros, Nick Faldo, Tiger Woods, Lorena Ochoa and Stacy Lewis are just some of the golfers to make their way across the bridge on their way to victory in Open Championships staged on the Old Course.

merchant and professional classes, particularly in the major burghs and coastal towns in the south and east of the country.[3]

The eighteenth century saw the first major steps towards the modern game, when golfing societies were formed, the rules began to be codified, fixed courses laid out and open competitions were held. The earliest club is thought to have been established by the Edinburgh Burgess Golfing Society in 1735 ('The Royal Burgess Golfing Society of Edinburgh' since 1929), whose members originally played on Bruntsfield Links on the south side of the town.[4] In 1744 the Company of Gentlemen Golfers ('The Honourable Company of Edinburgh Golfers' since 1800) drew up the 'Articles and Laws in Playing at Golf', a set of thirteen rules whose principles still underpin the game's current regulations.[5] The societies often adopted bright uniforms to warn other common land users of the players' approach.

Much of the sociable side of the early game was conducted in local inns and hotels. In the second half of the eighteenth century a number of 'Goffing Houses', or golf houses, were constructed at several locations including St Andrews (before 1766), Leith Links (1767–8), and at the east and west ends of Bruntsfield Links (before 1788).[6] The origins of the golf houses are not clear, but the Leith Links house (on the site of what is now the former Leith Academy Secondary School at Lochend Road) was certainly purpose-built from subscriptions by the Honourable Company of Edinburgh Golfers.[7] The 8-room house, with its bowling green, stable and garden, operated effectively as a tavern, leased to a professional inn-keeper as a tenant. Like the other clubs of the period, the Honourable Company was not officially incorporated as a 'legal society' or 'body corporate' until the early nineteenth century. A trustee held the property rights on behalf of the club, and the Links themselves were leased. By 1788 golf was considered *the* fashionable amusement in Edinburgh.[8] Club manufacturers and makers of the leather balls stuffed with feathers, known as 'featheries', clustered around these early golfing centres. There were at least eleven golfing societies formed in Scotland before 1800: Edinburgh Burgess Golfing Society (1735); Honourable Company of Edinburgh Golfers (1744); Bruntsfield Links Golfing Society (1761); Society of St Andrews Golfers, later the Royal and Ancient Golf Club (by 1766); Musselburgh Golf Club (by 1774); Fraserburgh Golf Club (by 1777); Society of Golfers at Aberdeen (1780); Crail Golfing Society (1786); Glasgow Golf Club (1787); Burntisland Golf Club (by 1791); and Cruden Golf Club (by 1791).

Some clubs appear to have struggled during the period of the Napoleonic Wars in the first years of the nineteenth century, and again following the financial crisis of 1825–6. Only a handful of new clubs were founded between 1800 and 1840. Most of these new societies comprised small numbers of members (between ten and thirty) and played existing, well-established, courses and used taverns, hotels or sometimes marquees for socialising and events. A few societies rented or bought existing properties at a short distance from the course to adapt as clubhouses, such as Royal Perth Golfing Society, which leased premises in Princes Street after its institution in 1824, then purchased 18 Charlotte Street in 1837.[9] Throughout the first half of the nineteenth century there was a slow, but steady, consolidation of the rules of the game and some technical innovations such as the introduction

The Golfers
by Charles Lees, 1847
National Galleries of Scotland, Edinburgh

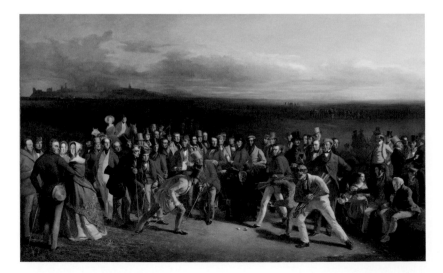

of hickory-shafted golf clubs in 1826 and a stand-ardised 4.25 inch hole-cutting machine, invented by Robert Grey at Musselburgh in 1828. In some places, such as Bruntsfield Links and Leith Links, the courses became overcrowded, and the old clubs moved further afield to more spacious sites.

The invention in 1848 by the Revd Dr Robert Adams Paterson of a cheap and durable molded gutta-percha ball, or 'guttie', impervious to damp and capable of mass production, transformed the sport.[10] Play now continued all year round, and irons came to the fore, with the ball being struck, rather than swept by the old longnose wooden playclubs. From 1850 the numbers of new societies rose significantly to an average of almost five a year in the 1870s, with several, such as Prestwick Golf Club, purchasing their own land for courses, while others shared existing courses and facilities. As the century progressed, a wider range of social groups formed their own clubs, such as the St Andrews Mechanics (workers, 1843), Montrose Mechanics (workers, 1847), the University of St Andrews (students, 1854), Monifieth (foundry artisans, 1858), Musselburgh Larks (workers before business hours, 1883), Lundin Mill (mill-workers, 1868), and Edinburgh Electric (telegraph department workers, 1883) amongst many other school, university and company clubs.[11]

The earliest surviving purpose-built clubhouse of the modern era appears to be that of the Royal and Ancient Golf Club in St Andrews, designed by the local architect George Rae in 1853 along the lines of a gentlemen's club with changing facilities for golfers.[12] Initially the clubhouse was constructed in a heavy neoclassical style, but as subsequent alterations and additions were made, a much lighter, brighter and informal type of struc-ture emerged with big bay windows, verandas and balconies enabling spectators to look out over the course. The model of the Royal and Ancient club-house spread relatively slowly in the subsequent two decades, and then mainly by the older and more affluent clubs. The Honourable Company built their own clubhouse on what is now Balcarres Road at the west end of Musselburgh Links in 1865; the Bruntsfield Links Golfing Society purchased an old Episcopal chapel in Millhill, Musselburgh in 1871, and then commissioned Hippolyte Jean Blanc to design a purpose-built clubhouse in Balcarres Road, Musselburgh, in 1885; Musselburgh Golf Club added their own clubhouse to Balcarres Road in 1873; and the Royal Burgess followed in 1875.[13]

From 1880 the pace of clubhouse construction quickened as increasing prosperity, improved trans-port and greater leisure time led to an explosion of interest in the game. Several hundred new clubs were founded and courses built from Machrihanish (Campbeltown) to Orkney between 1880 and the start of the First World War in 1914. In addition to the traditional coastal locations, clubs looked to new heathland and parkland venues to meet their needs, and a specialist discipline of golf course design emerged. Many of the new clubs built basic huts of corrugated iron or overlapping timber over a timber frame. Such buildings were advertised in the new specialist golfing press, and could be ordered from the catalogues of ironwork firms like Glasgow's Frederick Braby & Co., A. & J. Main & Co., Speirs &

Turnberry Hotel, designed by James Miller, 1904
Listed Category B
Photo: RCAHMS

Kingussie Golf Clubhouse, designed by Alexander Mackenzie, 1911
Listed Category C
Photo: RCAHMS

Cruden Bay Golf Club Starter's Box, Aulton Road, Cruden Bay, 1899
Listed Category C
Photo: Historic Scotland, Edinburgh

Co., or Walter MacFarlane & Co., transported to the nearest station, and erected by local contractors using numbered diagrams. Kilsyth Lennox Golf Club, founded in 1899, built a 'Wee Green Hut' of this type, and it was transported on the back of a cart to a new site when the club moved to its current location in 1905.[14] At the other end of the scale, some clubs commissioned architects to design clubhouses of considerable size and sophistication. Most clubhouses were conservative in their design, looking to historical models of domestic architecture to create a comfortable home from home for members. Large fireplaces, timber panelling and eclectic collections of homely furniture were typical. Such was the scale of the golfing enthusiasm that some clubs needed ancillary buildings including starter's boxes, caddie shelters, greenkeeper's houses and stabling and storage for course maintenance equipment.

Although the first golfing societies were all-male, the game itself was not confined to men. Famously the Earl of Moray accused Mary, Queen of Scots, of playing 'palmall and goif' in the grounds of Seton Palace shortly after the death of her husband, Lord Darnley, in 1567.[15] The Musselburgh Golf Club sponsored prizes of a creel, shawl and 'two of the best Barcelona silk handkerchiefs' for the best female golfer amongst the town's 'Fish Ladies' in 1811.[16] The first women's golf club, the Ladies' Golf Club of St Andrews (the Ladies' Putting Club since 1948) was formed in 1867, but restricted to the Himalayas putting course. Sixteen women's clubs formed by 1892, but almost all played on short courses separate from the men, and these were frequently shared with boys. Only in the 1890s did women's clubs begin to acquire their own 9- or 18-hole courses and clubhouses, such as: Machrihanish Ladies' Golf Club designed by H. E. Clifford in 1893; Carnoustie Ladies' Golf Club, built in 1895 by Dalhousie Estate architect David Fraser; the Troon Ladies' Golf Club of 1897, also designed by H.E. Clifford; Lundin Links designed by James Ross Gillespie in 1897 (subsequently moved in

MACHRIHANISH LADIES' CLUBHOUSE, ARGYLL AND BUTE, 1893
Photo: RCAHMS

Machrihanish Ladies' clubhouse appears to be one of the earliest, if not the first, purpose-built facility for women golfers in Scotland. The 'attractive and comfortable house occupying an excellent position opposite the home hole' was built in 1893. The architect is thought to be H.E. Clifford, who designed the nearby men's clubhouse in 1887.

GLENEAGLES HOTEL, AUCHTERARDER, PERTHSHIRE, 1910–24

Listed Category B
National Railway Museum / Science & Society Picture Library

Recognising the huge popularity of golf in the early years of the twentieth century, and perhaps rising to the challenge of the Glasgow and South Western Railway's Turnberry Hotel of 1906, Donald Matheson, the General Manager of the Caledonian Railway Company, decided to build a 'Scottish Resort of Distinction' with its own luxury hotel and railway station at Gleneagles in 1910. The intention was to offer a 'combination of the comforts and pleasures of the modern de-luxe and the delightful old country house, in such pleasant surroundings and with such facilities for rest and recreation indoors, that Gleneagles may well become the vogue, and thus be

confirmed in its becoming title "The Scottish Resort"'. The main draw was to be two magnificent moorland golf courses, the King's and Queen's Courses, designed by the noted player and golf course architect, James Braid. Other attractions included top-class tennis facilities, modelled on those at Wimbledon, and traditional field sports. Construction of the golf courses and the hotel, originally designed by James Miller in a late eighteenth-century neoclassical style, resumed after the First World War. The architect Matthew Adam and interior designer Charles W. Swanson completed the hotel for the London, Midland and Scottish Railway Company 'on the most modern principles' in time for a grand opening gala on 7 June 1924. Built using 'fireproof' concrete and steel, and faced with white Northumberland sandstone, the palatial hotel contained about 200 bedrooms and several enormous public rooms including a 70 feet by 40 feet ballroom with a specially sprung floor.

LMS GLENEAGLES HOTEL
PERTHSHIRE
BY NORMAN WILKINSON.

1909); or the former men's clubhouse taken on by the Ladies' Panmure Golf Club at Monifieth in 1898.[17] Shared premises began to flourish in the new century, for example the Cramond Brig clubhouse, designed by Murphy & Kinross in 1908, where the women's smaller clubroom and locker room were located above the men's accommodation and a separate ladies' veranda was provided.[18]

Landed family fortunes had begun to collapse before the First World War, and golf had benefitted by clubs leasing or acquiring and adapting parkland landscapes such as those at Duddingston House (1895), Killermont House (1904), Ranfurly Castle (1905), Kenmure House (1906) and Duff House (1910), but the trend accelerated after the sharp increase in death duties and income tax in 1918 with

Prestonfield House (1920), Prestongrange House (1922), Taymouth Castle (1925), Dalmahoy House (1927), Cawder House (1933) and Buchanan Castle (1936) among the notable examples. Very few new clubhouses were built between the wars or in the two decades after the Second World War, and those that were generally avoided the fashionable flat-roofed Modernist styles. Prominent exceptions include clubhouses at Musselburgh Golf Club, Monktonhall (1937, John Logan), Cardross Golf Club (1956), Silverknowes (1961–4, Alan Reiach & Partners), Carnoustie Municipal (1968, Victor Jackson) and Cambuslang (1971).

CARDROSS GOLF CLUBHOUSE, MAIN ROAD, CARDROSS, DUNBARTONSHIRE, 1956
Listed Category B
Photo: Cardross Golf Club

The old Cardross Golf Clubhouse was destroyed by German bombing on 5 May 1941, some attributing the random blitz to the night-time bombers mistaking the golf course greens for oil tanks. Unusually, the new clubhouse, which opened on 10 March 1956, looked back to the Art Deco style of the inter-war years with its streamlined, angular plan-form and communal rooms with large bowed windows facing north and west towards the golf course. The clubhouse is often mistakenly attributed to the celebrated modernist T.S. Tait, who had masterplanned the 1938 Empire Exibition in Glasgow in this sleek new style.

Highland Games
and Athletics

DONALD DINNIE WINDOW, HUNTLY ARMS HOTEL, ABOYNE, 1950
This stained glass window commemorates the extra-ordinary athlete and strong man, Donald Dinnie (1837–1916), who was widely considered the greatest Scottish athlete of the nineteenth century. He triumphed in over 11,000 competitions and Highland games for wrestling, running, long and high jumping, stone-putting, hammer-throwing and caber-tossing.

HIGHLAND GAMES

The tradition of Highland games is said to have originated with King Malcolm III (also known as Malcolm Canmore) in the eleventh century, who held competitions at the Brae of Mar as a method of selecting the ablest athletes to be soldiers and couriers. Highland games were held on a regular basis in the area surrounding Braemar by nearby clans, using it as a chance to meet and socialise. The games at Ceres in Fife are reputed to have taken place continuously (apart from war years) since 1314, when Robert the Bruce granted a charter to hold the games in celebration of the bowmen of the district who fought with him at the Battle of Bannockburn.[1] In the aftermath of the 1745 Jacobite Rising, the Act of Proscription was passed in 1746 to dismantle the clan system and outlaw Highland dress, customs and gatherings, such as Highland games. Piping competitions revived at the Falkirk Tryst in 1781 under the patronage of the Highland Society of London. Following the repeal of the Act in July 1782, there was a modern revival of gatherings, for example at Inverness (the Northern Meeting) in 1788. The St Fillans Highland Society organised full-scale games with piping, dancing and athletics in 1819.[2] In 1832 the Braemar Highland Society decided to give £5 for prizes at the gathering, and this marked the start of regulated competitions. Patronage of the landed gentry and aristocracy often played an important part in the staging of games, which were frequently accompanied by balls and other social gatherings. Queen Victoria first attended the Braemar Gathering in 1848. Continuing royal endorsement promoted the popular appeal of Highland games in general in the second half of the nineteenth century, with many new venues such as Pitlochry (1852), Ballater (1864), Comrie (1870), and Cowal at Dunoon (1894). The spectacle and competitions attracted very large numbers of spectators. By 1906, 12,000 people were attending the Crieff Highland Gathering.

Athletic competitions, including running, jumping and heavyweight events, such as hammer-throwing,

NORTHERN MEETING PARK GRANDSTAND, ARDROSS STREET, INVERNESS, 1865
Listed Category B
Photo: Historic Scotland, Edinburgh

The Northern Meeting Park Grandstand is thought to be the earliest and largest permanent structure associated with Highland games. Designed by the local firm of Matthews & Lawrie and opened for the September 1865 meeting, the 178-foot long by 34-foot wide stone-built stand accommodated 700 seats with 'a ladies' waiting room, gentlemen's room, competitors' room, two apartments for the keeper of the grounds, and two refreshment rooms' on the ground floor beneath. Half the seats were reserved for members of the Northern Meeting, and the other half were made available to the general public. Iron columns support the roof, and a decorative iron parapet railing runs along the length of the stand. Portable shutters were designed to enclose the stand in winter.

stone-putting, weight-throwing and caber-tossing, formed an integral part of the games. For the mostpart, games took place with temporary facilities and little or no permanent provision for spectators or participants. The nature of games or gatherings as annual events (subject to the vagaries of the weather) made, and continues to make, permanent sporting and spectating facilities a precarious investment for organisers.

The Northern Meeting was an early exception, firstly constructing its own rooms on the corner of Church Street and Baron Taylor's Street in Inverness for balls and piping competitions in 1789, then acquiring the Northern Meeting Park in 1864 and erecting the grandstand, or 'pavilion', there in the following year. St Fillans Highland Society constructed a hall in 1819.[3] Crieff, another of the larger games, leased Market Park from 1887 and

PATRON'S PAVILION AND STANDS AT THE PRINCESS ROYAL AND DUKE OF FIFE PARK, BRAEMAR, 1906
Listed Category C
Photo: Braemar Gathering Annual

Using the natural topography of the hollow at the Auchindryne end of the village, the Aberdeen architects and engineers, Jenkins & Marr, laid out the new twelve-acre ground on the site of the old curling ponds for the Braemar Royal Highland Society in 1906. At its heart lay the great oval games area, surrounded on three sides by a 60-foot wide gravelled 'promenade'. The north side of the oval was reserved for the grandstand and royal pavilion, now known as the Patron's Pavilion. Before the acquisition of a permanent site, the Braemar Games had a tradition of providing an elaborately decorated temporary pavilion for its royal visitors. This tradition continues at the new pavilion, which to this day is dressed with flags and sprigs of Scots fir and swags of purple heather rope for the annual gathering. The private enclosure, next to the Patron's Pavilion, was built in 1939, a year after the long, covered stand. Foot races have been staged at the gathering since 1832, making them the world's oldest organised races on a regular basis by the same body.

built a permanent stand in 1890 (destroyed by fire in the 1970s). The gathering at Braemar took place in various venues until it acquired a permanent home at the Princess Royal and Duke of Fife Park in 1906. As with horse-racing, the grandstands served to shelter spectators from the elements and to maximise views of the sporting field below through the use of stepped seating.

ATHLETICS

Athletics in various forms have a very long history in Scotland. The genesis of the modern athletic gathering took place in the sports of the revived Highland games and in the sports days of the universities, former pupil clubs and cricket clubs from the 1860s. The oldest continuous athletics meeting in Scotland belongs to the St Ronan's Border Games, which were established

DAM PARK STADIUM STAND, CONTENT AVENUE, AYR, 1959–63

Listed Category B
Photo: Ross Brown

Dam Park Stadium began life as the ground of Ayr Cricket Club in 1898. By the 1950s Ayr Town Council had begun to develop plans with the architects J. & J. A. Carrick for a new type of facility, a general purpose 'sports arena', at Dam Park. The first stage of the transformation was the construction of a championship standard seven-lane cinder running track in 1960–1. This was followed in 1962 by a replacement 650-seat grandstand with changing and catering facilities underneath. The Ayrshire Post dubbed the grandstand as 'do-it-yourself' because much of the design, quantity surveying and construction work was carried out by local men for a relatively modest £45,000. The home-made origins and budget price belied a technically adventurous and visually striking addition to Scotland's sporting buildings.

**DAM PARK STADIUM STAND,
CONTENT AVENUE, AYR, 1959–63**
Listed Category B
Photo: Ross Brown

Maurice Hickey of the Ayr Burgh Surveyor's Office designed the stand with F.A. Macdonald & Partners of Glasgow as consulting engineers and James Laidlaw & Sons as specialist concrete contractors. Eleven reinforced concrete ribs support a stepped stand and deeply cantilevered canopy, which allows unobstructed views out over the track. Deputations from sporting venues in the major cities, including Meadowbank in Edinburgh, visited to inspect the pioneering design and layout before the official opening on 25 May 1963. The first fully synthetic athletics track in the UK opened at Grangemouth three years later.

at Innerleithen in September 1827 for sprint, middle-distance racing, triple jump, high jump, long jump, shot-putt, hammer and wrestling.[4] Football and cycling clubs held their own general sports days from the 1870s, whichwere extremely popular, attracting large crowds and big fields of competitors for a wide range of events. Volunteer corps also held sports days. The formation of the Scottish Amateur Athletic Association (S.A.A.A.) on 26 February 1883 marked the start of formal athletic championships and regulation in Scotland.[5] The founder clubs were mostly drawn from the former pupil clubs and universities, along with the West of Scotland Football Club. The first championship took place at the recreation grounds for Edinburgh and Leith at Powderhall on 23 June 1883 in front of 3,000 people. The sports included sprints, hurdles, a half-mile, a mile, walking, pole-vaulting, high-jumping, long-jumping, the hammer, and the shot-putt.[6] From 1885 the first harrier clubs began to establish, starting with Clydesdale and Edinburgh. As facilities with the new sport of cycling were often shared, a close association with the Scottish Cyclists' Union (1889) and the Scottish Executive of the National Cyclists' Union developed.

From the 1870s, the three large Glasgow football clubs incorporated oval running and cycling tracks within their new stadia, and there were three cinder tracks in the east of Scotland (Powderhall, Northfield and Hawkhill), but dedicated athletics facilities remained rare outside the cities. The recreation grounds at Powderhall had opened on 1 January 1870 to cater for those with an interest in 'cricket, archery, pedestrianism, velocipede practice &c.'.[7] Over subsequent decades it came to be synonymous with athletics, and the facilities there grew to cater for that sport until 1923, when it became a greyhound track. Edinburgh Town Council constructed a new running track and pavilion at Meadowbank in 1932.[8] Hampden became the regular host of the Scottish Championships until 1951. After the Second World War an increasing number of dedicated athletics training and championship facilities were established. Ayr Town Council constructed a new championship standard cinder track at Dam Park in 1960, followed by an innovative grandstand and pavilion in 1962–3. The first fully synthetic track in Scotland was laid at Grangemouth in 1966. A major redevelopment of Meadowbank in preparation for the 1970 Commonwealth Games incorporated a pioneering indoor training concourse. The conversion of the Kelvin Hall in Glasgow in 1987 created the first permanent facility capable of hosting indoor competitions in Scotland.

Horse-racing

KELSO RACECOURSE MAIN STAND, 1822
Listed Category A
Photo: RCAHMS

The racecourse at Kelso has had three locations in its history. Sir Alexander Don first established the Kelso Races in 1751 at Caverton Edge, some five miles from the town, where according to James Haig, the 3rd Duke of Roxburghe built 'an elegant stand for the accommodation of the company, the lower part of which contained stables for the running horses, where they were kept during the races'. In 1818 the duke moved the course even further away to Blakelaw (Blaicklaw) in order to plant trees at Caverton (now Bowmont Forest). The old stand was demolished to placate local farmers, who complained about the nuisance of gypsy revels at the building. The Blakelaw course proved extremely unpopular with the townsfolk, who tried to burn the new planting at Caverton. Before a stand could be built, the course was moved again to Berrymoss, its current location, only a mile from the centre of Kelso.

On 12 July 1822 the duke laid the foundation stone for a new stand by an as yet unidentified architect.[179]

And sum, to schaw thare courtlie corsis
Wald ryid to Leith, and ryn thare horssis
And wychtlie wallope ouer the sandis.

Sir David Lyndsay, *The Complaynt of Schir David Lyndesay to the Kingis Grace*, 1529

William the Lion, King of Scots from 1165 to 1214, is traditionally believed to have established horse-racing at Lanark and gifted a silver bell to the town as a trophy. If true, the original bell was long lost or destroyed when it was replaced in 1608. James IV was a passionate horseman, keen on pageants, hunting, jousting and racing. He is known to have purchased horses from as far afield as Spain and Poland. The Lord High Treasurer's accounts show that Thomas Boswell, master of the King's wardrobe, paid eighteen shillings to the boy that 'ran the Kingis hors' at Leith on 15 April 1504.[1] James IV's successors were also keen patrons of the turf, notably the enthusiastic James VI and I, who established Newmarket in England as a horse-racing centre following his accession to the English throne.

Horse-races were taking place at Leith by 1504, Haddington by 1552, Peebles by 1574, Ayr by 1576, Stirling by 1598, Glasgow by 1606, Paisley in 1608, Dunfermline and Cupar by 1610, Dumbarton by 1615, Perth (South Inch) in 1613, Jedburgh by 1625, and Irvine (Bogside) by 1636, but the meetings were sporadic at some venues.[2] The nature of the seventeenth-century races differed significantly from modern-day racing – there were no written rules, no standardised distances, no grandstands, the courses were marked with wooden distance posts, and there were various types of racing, including 'matches' between just two horses.

The sport was suppressed as a potential hotbed of Royalist agitation by Oliver Cromwell's Protectorate, but resumed with a new fervour as 'The Sport of Kings' under the racing enthusiast Charles II at the Restoration of the monarchy in 1660. Aberdeen and Berwick-upon-Tweed (Lamberton, on the Scottish side of the border) started racing in 1661, Inverness and Dumfries in

LANARK SILVER BELL, 1608
Royal Burgh of Lanark Museum Trust

Silver bells were the commonest form of early trophy in horse-racing. The form of the trophy is believed to derive from the ancient practice of decorating horses with bells and ribbons on the 1st May. The earliest known silver bell trophies are the Carlisle Bells of 1590 and 1597, which are of circular jingle-bells type, rather than open-ended. The winner was expected to add an engraved medal recording the victory to the original trophy. Silver bell trophies were contested in Scotland at Lanark,

Paisley, Glasgow, Dunfermline and Haddington. Robert Denneistoun or Henry Lindsay of Edinburgh made a new Lanark Silver Bell in 1608, which remains the sport's oldest trophy in Scotland. Although the race was discontinued at Lanark in 1977, the series was revived at Hamilton in 2008, and a new silver bell created by Hamilton & Inches of Edinburgh in 2012.

1662, Banff by 1684, and North Berwick and Huntly by 1695.[3] In most cases the races were run on flat common land, moorland, links land or beaches, where there was room for the course and crowds of spectators. Often the royal burghs encouraged the sport by presenting a trophy, to which tokens were added with the winners' names. The races brought prestige and accompanying commerce to the host burgh. Some prize races were restricted to the work-horses of the burgh, while others were open to the racehorses belonging to the aristocracy and gentry of the county.[4] Local farm-horse races, which were associated with events such as fairs, feast days, common ridings or even marriages (the 'broose') in smaller towns and villages were also widespread in the seventeenth and eighteenth centuries.

Leith Races, which were run around distance posts on the beach, remained the largest and most popular meetings in the first half of the eighteenth century, while other venues seem to have declined. By the second half of the eighteenth century the increase in population of the burghs placed pressure on the common lands, and many meetings had gained bad reputations for their accompanying gambling, drinking, rowdiness and even violence. On 2 August 1777 the Dukes of Hamilton, Buccleuch, Roxburgh and Gordon formed a new field sports and horse-racing society, the Hunters' Club, later known as the Caledonian Hunt, then the Royal Caledonian Hunt. This elite group patronised existing meetings in different locations each year and discouraged excessive drinking and banned gambling. The prestige of the Royal Caledonian Hunt meetings helped to inject a new energy and respectability into the sport. New venues, such as Ayr (1771) and Hamilton (1782), emerged and the first permanent facilities for racing were built, in many cases on privately owned sites at a little distance from the town centre. The Duke of Roxburghe constructed one of the first combined stand and racecourse stables at Caverton Edge for the Kelso races in the last quarter of the eighteenth century.[5]

The Napoleonic Wars of 1803–15 appear to have

disrupted participation in the sport, and a number of courses struggled. After several locations were considered for re-siting Leith Races, including on The Meadows in Edinburgh, they transferred to a new course at Musselburgh in 1816.[6] Such was the daily exodus to Musselburgh from Edinburgh that the magistrates ordered the early opening of Waterloo Place and Regent Road in 1819 to accommodate the traffic, and spectators gathered on Calton Hill to watch the crowds returning.[7] By the 1820s the courses themselves appear to have been marked-out more formally, and all the venues detailed on Wood's town plans of that decade show elongated oval circuits (e.g. Aberdeen, Montrose, Perth North Inch). Newer courses on private lands marked on the Ordnance Survey maps of the 1850s seem to adopt a more rectangular plan, perhaps to minimise disturbance to the existing field pattern. Hamilton alone, had a large L-plan circuit in a crook of the River Clyde. Permanent stands, or 'view houses' were still relatively uncommon in the early nineteenth century, but by the middle of the century there were a few, usually funded by subscriptions, including those at Airdrie (1850s), Ayr, Glasgow Kelvinside, Irvine Bogside, Kelso Berrymoss (1822), Musselburgh (about 1820), and Perth North

PERTH RACECOURSE MAIN STAND, 1910
Listed Category B

Perth races moved from the North Inch to Scone Palace Park in September 1908. Donald McIntosh, clerk of works to the Mansfield estates, designed the new stand in 1910 for the Perth Hunt Committee and the Earl of Mansfield. The *Dundee Courier* described the works:

The stand is constructed of an iron frame clad on the outside with timber. The main platform is supported on heavy iron beams, the steps or tiers consisting of teak wood. It is 72 feet long. On the ground floor there is a luncheon room and kitchen, members' bar, and public bar. On the upper flat there is a large lunch and tea room, 55 feet by 17 feet, as well as a ladies' cloakroom, stewards' room, and balcony. The addition presents a really bright and pleasing appearance. The outside timber is treated throughout with carbolicium. The ironwork has been painted a pretty pale blue, while the balustrading and handrails are white.[181]

The previous year a pavilion had been constructed in the paddock for the clerk of the course, press, jockeys, police, telegraph office and weighing room. The stand was extended in a similar style in 1954.

Inch (1806). The 13th Earl of Eglinton was an avid supporter of horse-racing, amongst other sports, promoting the first recorded steeplechase in Scotland at his Bogside course on 25 April 1839.[8]

With consolidation of rules for the sport and an increasingly centralised UK-wide regulation (and eventually licensing) of flat-racing through the Jockey Club and steeplechase through the National Hunt Committee, the second half of the nineteenth century saw a consolidation of elite horse-racing to a smaller number of locations.[9] *The Racing Calendar* for 1869 recorded eleven racecourses in Scotland: Airdrie, Ayr, Musselburgh, Irvine, Glasgow Kelvinside, Hawick, Kelso, Lamberton, Lanark, Paisley and Perth. Apart from regulation, the venues were influenced by publications on the layout of racecourses and their buildings, such as Richard Darvill's influential *Treatise on the Care, Treatment, and Training of English Race Horses* and Delabere P. Blaine's *An Encyclopaedia of Rural Sports*, which offered advice on matters including the design of stands, betting rooms, saddling, weighing and rubbing houses, and stabling. Some of the more flourishing venues, such as Ayr, constructed quite large multipurpose buildings to house the spectators, officials and jockeys. 'View House', still surviving at Doonfoot Road, Ayr, was designed by James I. McDerment in 1867, and forms part of the old racecourse stand, originally containing refreshment, jockeys' and reporters' rooms on the ground floor and ladies' and smoking rooms above.[10]

Edward VII's passion for horse-racing brought

Musselburgh Racecourse Stand, detail of roof
ventilators, 1886
Listed Category C

Eglinton Stand entrance, Ayr Racecourse,
Whitletts Road, Ayr, 1963

Musselburgh Racecourse Stand
Listed Category C
Photo: Historic Scotland, Edinburgh

a renewed interest in the sport in the early years
of the twentieth century. The sporting public
required an increasing level of comfort and sophistication, which was reflected in new facilities at
racecourses. The new course at Ayr opened in
Wallacetown on 18 September 1907. The layout of
the course and the original club stand was by W.C.
& A.S. Manning of Newmarket, but executed by
Allan Stevenson. As a symbol of the male-dominated establishment that refused to allow women
to vote, the original stand was burnt by the suffragette Kate Taylor in 1913, and rebuilt in 1913–15.[11]
At Kelso too, the suffragette Arabella Scott was
convicted in April 1913 for her attempt to set fire
to the stand.[12] The First World War put a halt to
racing, and many courses struggled to re-open.
Lanark, Hamilton and Musselburgh invested in
major new stands in this period. The Second World
War similarly disrupted racing, and the difficult
post-war decades were to prove terminal to the
sport at Lanark and Irvine Bogside. Only briefly
in the late 1960s was there sufficient demand and
financial stability for additional facilities at Ayr and
Kelso, aided by the beginning of commercial sponsorship and the Horserace Betting Levy Board.
New investment and technology in the 1980s
started a renaissance in the popularity of the sport,
which has continued to the present day at Ayr,
Hamilton, Kelso, Musselburgh and Perth.

The design of racecourse stands and associated buildings was a relatively specialist field,
dominated by a small number of architectural firms.
Allan Stevenson worked on numerous schemes for
Irvine Bogside (1883; 1895–6; 1899; 1906; 1910;
1913; 1917; 1921–2), Ayr (1907; club stand, 1913);
and Musselburgh (1886). His firm merged with
Carricks to become Carricks Harley Hay in 2007.
Carricks also had a history of designing racecourse
buildings, including the Eglinton Stand at Ayr,
1963–71, and the stables, hostel and possibly the
new stand at Kelso in 1968–9.[13] Harold Oswald, an
architect from Newcastle-upon-Tyne was another
significant racing architect, working at Lanark,
Hamilton and Musselburgh in the 1920s.[14]

HAMILTON PARK RACECOURSE WEIGHING–IN ROOM, 1926
Listed Category C

Racing had taken place sporadically in the parklands of Hamilton Palace since at least 1782. Sir Loftus Bates, Col Robertson-Aikman and Lord Hamilton of Dalzell moved the racecourse to its current location in 1926, when racing was revived after a 19-year break. Harold Oswald of Newcastle-upon-Tyne designed a suite of new buildings in 1926, including this weighing room.

Ice Skating and
Ice Hockey

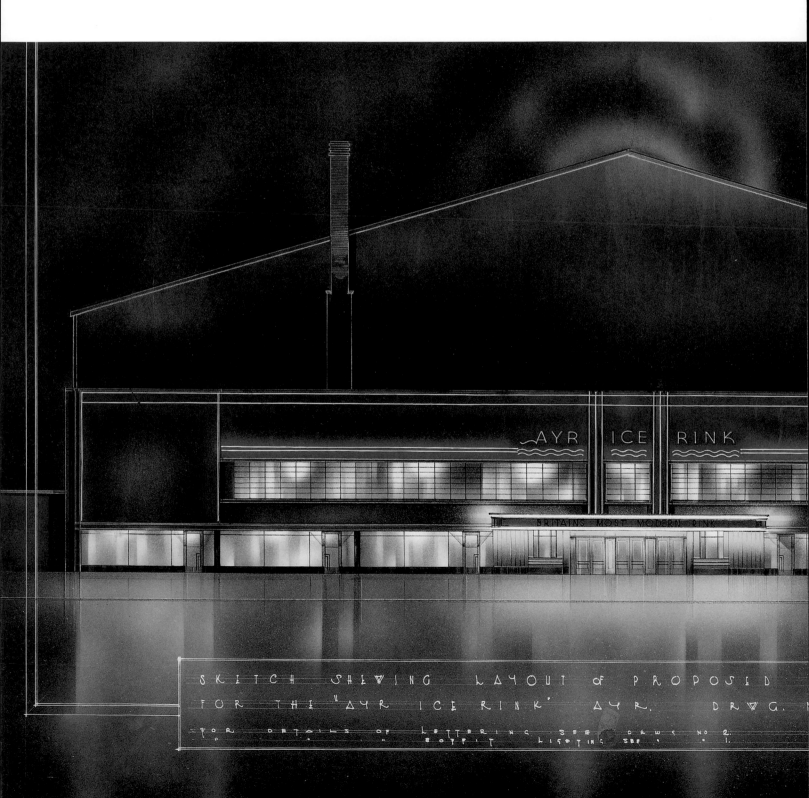

AYR ICE RINK

BRITAINS MOST MODERN RINK

SKETCH SHEWING LAYOUT OF PROPOSED
FOR THE "AYR ICE RINK" AYR. DRWG.
FOR DETAILS OF LETTERING SEE DRWS NO 2.
" " " SOFFIT LIGHTING SEE " " 1.

DESIGN FOR AYR ICE RINK, BERESFORD TERRACE, AYR, 1937
Photo: RCAHMS

The bright welcoming streamlined entrance and coloured neon-tube strips of J. & J.A. Carrick's design for the night-time illumination of Ayr Ice Rink reflect the Jazz Moderne glamour of contemporary North American rinks. The rink was demolished in 1972.

The contribution of the Edinburgh Skating Club so early in the real story of figure-skating cannot be over-estimated. It was the first organizing body that disciplined and guided skating into the right channels and popularized its practice among a wider circle.

Nigel Brown, *Ice-Skating*, London 1959, pp.37–9

The fast, long-distance form of was certainly popular in the Low Countries in the seventeenth century. Both Samuel Pepys and John Evelyn recorded skating for the first time in 1662 on the River Thames in London, where it was probably practised by returning exiles after the Restoration of Charles II. In spite of close trading and academic links with Holland, it was not until the eighteenth century that the sport caught on in Scotland, and then only in the form of figure skating. The precise date of the earliest skating in Scotland is not known, but the records of the Edinburgh Skating Club begin in 1784, and the club is believed to have been in existence for at least thirty years before that.[1] The thirty-nine members in 1784 were mainly landowners, lawyers, merchants or bankers and professional men, including a surgeon-dentist, three army officers, a bookseller and the architect of Edinburgh's George Square and Buccleuch Street, James Brown. Although women were not explicitly barred from what was frequently described as a 'manly and healthy recreation', the rules clearly envisaged a gentlemen's club.[2] Unlike the curlers, no permanent structure was required for storing equipment, so the skaters made do with tents beside Duddingston Loch and Lochend Loch and socialised in various hostelries in town. It was only late in the nineteenth century that shelters for the skaters were constructed beside Duddingston Loch.[3] Men were hired to sweep the ice of snow and an officer was employed to 'watch' the ice, which involved ensuring it was safe to use, charging non-members for use of the swept area, selling refreshments and ensuring ladders and ropes were on hand in case of accidents. A military band occasionally provided music for the skaters.

MURRAYFIELD ICE RINK, 13 RIVERSDALE CRESCENT, EDINBURGH, 1938–9
Listed Category B
Photo: RCAHMS

Designed by J.B. Dunn & Martin and completed on the eve of the Second World War in 1939 at a cost of £65,000 and with a seating capacity of 3,300, Murrayfield was the largest and most elaborate of the inter-war ice rinks. Although ready to open in 1939, the rink was requisitioned by the government as a Royal Army Service Corp depot for some years, and later used as a store. After considerable public and newspaper pressure, and some alterations, it finally opened to the public on 7 August 1952. The rink was bankrupt by 1957, at which point it was taken over by the current owners, who have kept it in use since, predominantly for skating and hockey, but also as a venue for ice shows, curling, boxing, basketball, speedway and musical events.

Skating undoubtedly took place in many locations around the country, but for many years the Edinburgh Skating Club was the only skating club in Scotland, and indeed in the UK. The Kelso Skating Club was instituted in February 1814, and in 1830 the Glasgow Skating Club met for the first time at the Petershill pond.[4] Other burghs followed throughout the nineteenth century, but relatively few skating clubs (e.g. Ayr at Castlehill, about 1890, and Paisley at Lochfield, 1891) built their own pavilions. That the sport was well-established in the Highlands by the mid-nineteenth century is reflected in the 1848 proposal for a skating and cricket club in Inverness.[5] Thomas Clay's *Instructions on the Art of Skating* of 1828 introduced combination figure skating, which was described by the Glasgow club president George Anderson in 1852: 'The object is to combine various movements in any arrangement agreed on, so timed that all the skaters, working from one common centre, interweave the figures and circles without collision, and when this is skilfully done the effect is beautiful.' The manoeuvres were shouted by a caller, and took place around a wooden marker. A National Skating Association was formed in Cambridge in 1879 to deal with malpractices in the Fens, where betting skewed results. Figure skating came under the control of the association in the following year. Towards the end of the nineteenth century the lack of certainty about freezing conditions on natural ponds and lochs, the increasing cost of maintaining safe outdoor rinks, and the need for longer practice sessions led to experiments with artificial curling rinks, and eventually to indoor skating.

A small indoor surface was achieved in London in 1840, and larger 'glaciariums' appeared from 1876 with the application of new commercial-scale refrigeration technology. Remnants of Scotland's first short-lived glaciarium survive in the O2 ABC Building at 304–332 Sauchiehall Street, Glasgow. Originally built as a great steel and glass-domed Diorama in 1875, and then used as a Panorama, the building was lavishly converted by the architect James Miller to become the 'Most Superb Ice Surface in Europe' as the Glasgow Real Ice Skating Palace in 1896.[6] The main attraction was ice skating, but on 2 June 1896 the first indoor curling match took place, and on 3 July a demonstration match of the new Canadian sport, ice hockey, was held.[7] In spite of the high expectations, and the additional excitement of the first cinematic

The Reverend Robert Walker Skating, **by Sir Henry Raeburn, about 1795**
National Galleries of Scotland, Edinburgh

Traditionally attributed to the painter Sir Henry Raeburn, this most famous work of Enlightenment Edinburgh depicts Robert Walker, minister of the Canongate Kirk, anti-slavery campaigner and member of the Edinburgh Skating Club, in action on the ice, probably at Duddingston Loch. Walker's severe expression, black garments and stiff pose have often been taken to characterise the moral rectitude and dour Presbyterianism of the contemporary kirk. The son of the minister of the Scots Kirk in Rotterdam, Walker was a keen and accomplished skater. He is depicted in the position for 'travelling on the outside edge', used by the Dutch for distance skating, as described in Robert Jones' *Treatise on Skating* of 1772.

film-show in Glasgow in May 1896, the Palace closed the following year. The building has undergone many uses and reconfigurations since, notably as Hengler's Circus from 1904, then as a cinema in 1929, and now as an entertainment venue.[8]

Scotland's first purpose-built indoor ice rink was constructed by the Scottish Ice Rink Company at Crossmyloof, Glasgow, in 1907. It represented a huge leap forward in technology and design from the circular rink of the old glaciarium in Sauchiehall Street, and was a forerunner to the internationally important Manchester Ice Palace of 1910. Built in the form of a large industrial shed with an arcaded elevation facing Titwood Road, the rectangular plan accommodated six curling sheets with room for spectators at ground level and on a balcony. Less practical were the roof columns that ran through the middle of the ice surface, one of which housed a bandstand just above head-height of

the skaters.[9] Crossmyloof Ice Rink was a great success, attracting the first international ice hockey match between Scotland and England in 1909, and a number of curling clubs. After a period of requisition for engineering use during the First World War, Watson, Salmond & Gray reconstructed and extended the building in 1928 to remove the interrupting central columns and provide greater spectator space for ice hockey. Crossmyloof Ice Rink was demolished in 1986.

In the 1890s there had been a short-lived fad for roller-skating and roller-hockey, imported from the United States, but improved skates and skating surfaces launched a second craze from 1908 to 1910. From Dumfries to Wick, joint-stock companies were formed to construct rinks for roller-skating.[10] The American Roller Rink at Russell Road, Murrayfield in Edinburgh, which opened on 31 July 1908, had a 30,000 ft2 maplewood floor 'the

Dundee Ice Rink, Kingsway West, Dundee, 1937–8
Photo: RCAHMS

Decorations in granolithic in the entrance vestibule at the former Dundee Ice Rink, which was demolished in 1993.

largest, smoothest and best in the world', and seats for 2,500 spectators.[11] Within two years the bubble had burst and the craze was over. Many rinks closed or were converted to cinemas or entertainment halls before the First World War.

Apart from Crossmyloof, a number of other ice rinks opened before the First World War, including one at Elgin designed by Robert Baillie Pratt in 1909 and the Haymarket Ice Rink in Edinburgh of 1912. The rinks were closed or severely curtailed during the First World War and the Depression of the 1920s, and it took many years for most of them to recover. Skating and curling continued to dominate the ice time, but fast and exciting ice hockey gathered significant momentum as a spectator sport, perhaps bolstered by importing star players from Canada. Undoubtedly the key event that sparked a frenzy of ice rink construction in the late 1930s was the sensational last-minute triumph of the Great Britain ice hockey team over the Canadians at the 1936 Winter Olympic Games at Garmisch-Partenkirchen in Bavaria. With the encouragement of town councils across Scotland, commercial companies formed to capitalise on the enormous popular enthusiasm for ice hockey. New rinks included: Perth (1936); Aberdeen (T. Scott Sutherland, 1937); Ayr (J. & J.A. Carrick, 1937–8); Dundee (William Mollison Wilson, 1937–8); Kirkcaldy (Williamson & Hubbard, 1937–8); Paisley (Frank Burnet & Boston, 1937–9); Dunfermline (John Fraser & Son, 1938–9); Falkirk (Wilson & Wilson, 1938); and Murrayfield, Edinburgh (J.B. Dunn & Martin, 1938–9). Like the earlier glaciaria, the new generation of ice rinks straddled the divide between sporting venues and entertainment halls, needing to maximise income from a variety of sources to cover high maintenance and operating costs. What mattered was size, both in terms of the ice surface for skating, curling and ice hockey, but most importantly for spectators were associated enticements such as lounges, restaurants, milk bars and shops. As a building type, ice rinks followed the model of the other major mass indoor entertainment venues, the cinemas. Little architectural effort went into the great ice barns, but most had welcoming, fashionably bright and colourful Art Deco or Jazz Moderne entrances, some illuminated by sleek neon striplights at night. The ice rinks were products of the golden age of the motor car, and where possible catered to their clients by providing huge car parks adjacent to the building. Typically just under a quarter of the cost of the building was spent on the refrigeration plant and the super-chilled concrete slab that hosted the ice. Almost all the new venues drew in existing curling clubs from a wide surrounding area and spurred the creation of local ice hockey teams, such as the Fife Flyers, Dundee Tigers, Perth Panthers, Falkirk Lions and Glasgow Mustangs. Unfortunately the outbreak of the Second World War in 1939 ended the ice rink craze as abruptly as it had begun, with some rinks in an unfinished state, and others closed for the duration of the war.

In spite of renewed interest in skating, curling and ice hockey after the war, ice rinks were not on the government's priority list for building permits, as Aberdeen discovered in the case of its rink, which had been damaged by the crash of a German bomber. The huge size of the venues, increasing health and safety, environmental and access requirements, and their high operating costs made ice rinks particularly vulnerable to the post-war economic cycles. With the exception of Falkirk (now an indoor football centre), Kirkcaldy and Murrayfield, all the pre-war ice rinks were demolished by the 1990s. Mostly driven by curling enthusiasts, new rinks were constructed in the 1960s and 1970s (e.g. Border Ice Rink, Kelso, 1964; Lockerbie, 1966; Hamilton, 1967; Stranraer, 1970), but all have required major refurbishments and some have been replaced altogether in the last twenty years. There are currently nineteen ice rinks operating throughout Scotland.

FIFE ICE ARENA, ROSSLYN STREET, KIRKCALDY, 1937–8
Listed Category B

A number of local businessmen formed a company in 1937 to plan a new ice rink for Kirkcaldy. A former assistant to Sir Robert Lorimer, Harry Hubbard of Williamson & Hubbard, designed the £38,000 building, which was planned to hold 4,000 spectators for ice hockey and to accommodate six curling rinks. A feature of the design was the ability to use the building as an entertainment hall when the floor area was not flooded. Although the bulk of the building comprises a utilitarian shed for the rink, the white-rendered entrance is marked by Art Deco details of streamlined fins and grilles in contrasting colours.

Rugby

THE GREENYARDS STAND, MELROSE RUGBY FOOTBALL CLUB, 1923

Melrose butchers, Ned Haig and David Sanderson, conceived the game of rugby sevens as a fundraising event for Melrose Rugby Football Club in 1883. It is now an official Olympic sport, and will be played at the Rio de Janeiro Games in 2016. The Greenyards ground is famous as the first rugby sevens venue, and continues to host the Melrose Sevens tournament. The *Southern Reporter* was keen to praise Melrose in the move to upgrade their Victorian legacy in 1923: 'I will say that the Melrose Rugby officials have earned my undying gratitude for demolishing their late unlamented pavilion. Melrose now possess the grandest stand in the South of Scotland, and they have apparently given the impetus to further stand-building.' The stand was further expanded to the north and south in the later twentieth century.

Rugby football is a game I can't claim absolutely to understand in all its niceties, if you know what I mean. I can follow the broad, general principles, of course. I mean to say, I know that the main scheme is to work the ball down the field somehow and deposit it over the line at the other end and that, in order to squalch this programme, each side is allowed to put in a certain amount of assault and battery and do things to its fellow man which, if done elsewhere, would result in 14 days without the option, coupled with some strong remarks from the Bench.

P.G. Wodehouse, *Very Good, Jeeves*, London, 1930

The history of rugby football in Scotland is largely entwined with the other forms of football until the decisive split between the feet-only game and the handling game with the formation of the Scottish Football Union (rugby) and the Scottish Football Association (soccer) in March 1873.[2] Unlike England, where rugby further subdivided into rugby union (amateur) and rugby league (professional) in 1895, the sport in Scotland remained predominantly under the rules of the Scottish Football Union until the 1980s.

Handling forms of football were played in a number of Edinburgh and Glasgow schools in the first half of the nineteenth century. A primitive form of rugby may have been played at Edinburgh Academy in 1851.[3] Two brothers from Durham School, Francis and Alexander Crombie, are said to have brought knowledge of Rugby School's 1845 'Rules of Rugby Football' when they moved to the Academy in 1854. Edinburgh's Royal High School adopted the first incomplete Rugby School rules in 1856. The Edinburgh Academical Football Club was certainly in existence by December 1857, when they won a rugby-like football game against the University of Edinburgh Football Club, but it was January 1858 before the club was formally constituted.[4] Although the location of the match is not identified, it is likely that it took place at the Academy's cricket ground at Raeburn Place in Stockbridge. Other early, mainly academic

or former pupil, rugby football clubs included Merchistonian Football Club (1858), St Salvator Football Club (University of St Andrews, 1858), West of Scotland Football Club (Partick, 1865), Glasgow Academical Football Club (1866) and Glasgow University Football Club (1869). Disputes and mix-ups over the rules were frequent until the clubs agreed to abide by 'The Green Book' in 1868, and then five years later founded the Scottish Football Union.[5]

Scotland won the first international match against England at the Edinburgh Academicals' Raeburn Place ground on 27 March 1871. The English team played all in white, with red roses on their shirts, and the Scotland team wore white cricket flannels and brown shirts with a thistle motif. The Calcutta Cup (Scotland versus England) was also first played at Raeburn Place in 1879. In 1883 the first Rugby Sevens competition was played at the Greenyards ground of Melrose Rugby Club. Many of the early club stands were constructed of timber.

MURRAYFIELD RUGBY STADIUM, EDINBURGH, 1992–4
Photo: RCAHMS

The name 'Murrayfield' is synonymous around the world with the home of Scottish Rugby. The original Murrayfield Stadium (above) was built on the same site in 1925, on nineteen acres of land originally belonging to the Edinburgh Polo Club. In response to the 1990 Taylor Report on stadium design, the Scottish Rugby Union commissioned a new all-seater bowl stadium (right) from the Miller Partnership (now Holmes Miller). It opened in phases between 1992 and 1994, and was built at a cost of £50 million, funded by a debenture scheme. The new stadium, capable of seating 67,500 spectators, opened with a match between Scotland and South Africa in November 1994.

Swimming and Aquatic Sports

ROYAL COMMONWEALTH POOL, DALKEITH ROAD, EDINBURGH, 1970
Listed Category A
Photo: Buro Happold

The 'Commie' was designed by Sir Robert Matthew, Johnson-Marshall & Partners (architects) in association with Arups (engineers) and Steensen Varming Mulcahy (service engineers) in 1967 as the main swimming and diving venue for the Commonwealth Games which were held in Edinburgh in 1970. The architect John Richards, later described the priorities for the building: 'it should serve as the hub of a system of teaching pools in Edinburgh after the Games; the building should take advantage of views to Arthur's Seat'. Built into a sloping site on Dalkeith Road, an ingenious arrangement of overlapping planes keeps the profile of the building clean and low. A major refurbishment in 2009–12, designed by S. & P Architects with Buro Happold (structural and service engineers), prepared the building as a training venue for the 2012 Olympics and as a training and diving venue for the 2014 Commonwealth Games.

In terms of natural positive feeling, I don't think anything will match touching the pool wall first in July 1976

David Wilkie on winning the gold medal at the Olympic Games in Montreal in July 1976

Public swimming pools have a relatively short history in Scotland. While bath-houses for thera-peutic or cleansing purposes, such as those at Bearsden, Bothwellhaugh, Cramond and Inchtuthil, date back to Roman times, pools for swimming and diving as recreation, exercise or sport only began to flourish in the last thirty years of the nineteenth century. While humane societies had been set up in the late eighteenth century to improve the appalling record of drowning accidents at sea and in lochs, rivers and canals, the establishment of pools created the first safe places for large numbers of people to learn to swim.

INDOOR POOLS

'Bagnios', or public baths for therapeutic purposes, flourished in the late seventeenth and eighteenth centuries, and the late eighteenth and early nine-teenth centuries saw the construction of private 'subscription baths' for middle and upper class patrons, but the swimming facilities were usually restricted to small plunge pools. Increasing concern for the health and hygiene of the working classes throughout the nineteenth century led to the establishment of large bath houses with individual 'slipper baths' (baths in the shape of a slipper, with a higher end for supporting the head) and clothes-washing facilities. A number of these bath-houses were reconstructed or expanded from the 1870s by the addition of swimming 'ponds' in an attempt to mix leisure and health with hygiene. Scotland's pools were distinguished by opening all year round, unlike their counterparts in England and Wales, which were often converted for gymnasium use in the winter.[1] Funding for construction of public baths and pools in the smaller burghs relied to a great extent on donations and benefactions from local landowners, individuals and businesses. Baths and

PORTOBELLO SWIM CENTRE, 57 PROMENADE, BELLFIELD STREET, PORTOBELLO, 1898–1901
Listed Category A
Photo: RCAHMS

The construction of public baths was a stipulation of the act to amalgamate the Burgh of Portobello with the City and Royal Burgh of Edinburgh in 1896. Designed by Edinburgh's City Architect, Robert Morham, and his deputy, James Anderson Williamson, the flagship building contained men's and ladies' ponds, with second-class single baths in the dividing section between them (now changing rooms), a Turkish baths suite, and a gymnasium, and a reading room, smoking area and refreshment room in the upper floors. Concerned not to repeat the plain design of the Infirmary Street Baths in the prominent position on Portobello's Promenade, the town council ordered a more ornate architectural treatment and Turkish baths to rival those of Dundee and Aberdeen, but sought to offset some of the additional costs by using free filtered salt water from the Firth of Forth rather than piped fresh water. The baths are no longer supplied with salt water, but the original inlet can still be seen at low tide.

wash-house legislation in Scotland was first incorporated into the Burgh Police Act (for urban areas) of 1892 and the Local Government (Scotland) Act (for rural areas) of 1894.[2]

Like many aspects of Victorian life, bathing and swimming was segregated by gender. This was often reflected in the design of the buildings and provision of facilities: separate male and female entrances, changing areas, baths and even pools. The entrances to Aberdeen's Public Baths (baths from 1851, pool added 1869) were in different streets: women entered from St Andrew Street and men from Crooked Lane. Of Glasgow's seven public pools by 1900, five had separate women's pools, which were all just over half the size of the men's pools (mainly 75 feet by 40 feet).[3] The number of slipper baths and times for associated Turkish (hot dry rooms) and Russian (steam) baths also favoured the men. Often facilities enforced segregation by specifying separate days and times for male and female swimming. Again, these arrangements were designed to cater primarily for male swimmers, with women allocated shorter hours at less busy periods. In some cases segregation was also by class, for example the expanded Dundee Corporation Baths of 1871, which had first, second and third class swimming pools of varying sizes, finishes, and cycles of water changes.[4] The public pools of the largest burghs, Edinburgh and Glasgow, were aimed specifically for the benefit of the working classes, so class segregation effectively took place by location. Private pools, such as the Arlington (1871), Western (1878) and Victoria (1878) in Glasgow and Drumsheugh (1882) and Warrender (1887) in

Edinburgh, similarly class-segregated their clientele by dint of their location in affluent areas and the ability of their mercantile and professional patrons to pay the subscriptions.[5]

Advances in construction and service technology enabled the provision of these larger pools in the late nineteenth century. In terms of external appearance, the municipal architects tended to look to the example of railway stations, which often had smart Italianate offices facing the street and large unornamented sheds behind. Internally, the pool halls were notable for their broad open roof structures of timber or iron and later steel. Glazing was almost always incorporated into the roof, either as a continuous cupola, or in strips along the roof slopes, to light the pool. Various methods were tried to achieve the best level of daylight and ventilation, and the minimum level of glare for swimmers. Artificial lighting in the early pool buildings was entirely by gas, which added to the problems of vapour and odour. The pools themselves were all rectangular and often varied in depth from about 3 or 4 feet at the shallow end to between 6 and 7 feet at the deep end. Cost-cutting at Perth in 1887 left a raw Portland cement surface without tiling to the bottom of the pool, but in most cases all the pool surfaces were covered with either glazed or enamel tiles.[6] Rounded corners were thought to improve the ability to clean the white tiles of the pools thoroughly.[7] Changing cubicles, often of teak to resist rot, were arranged around the outside of the pool. Some pool halls extended to two storeys, allowing a gallery level for additional changing cubicles, viewing,

SPIERS CENTRE, PRIMROSE STREET, ALLOA, 1898
Listed Category A
Photo: RCAHMS

Donated to the town by the worsted manufacturer, John Thomson Paton, the Alloa Baths and Gymnasium formed some of the most opulent public sporting facilities of their day. The £40,000 capital and £3,000 revenue endowments were augmented by annual subscriptions for private use of the building during a set period of the day, and entrance fees from the general public for use at other times. Apart from the 75 feet by 32 feet pool, the building contained billiards and amusements rooms, first and second class plunge baths, Turkish and Russian baths, as well as a wash-house and laundry. The architects were John Burnet, Sons & Campbell of Glasgow, who researched English and Scottish pools to ensure the latest technology, including electric lights, and the highest quality of construction and detailing. The exterior of the building, in a free French Renaissance style, is of richly decorated red sandstone with statues and sculpted low-relief panels. Similarly the interior was lavishly decorated with striped and chequered maroon and cream tiles, polished granite columns, ornate ironwork, and a series of dragons' heads to the hammerbeams of the pool hall roof. The striped and chequered tiling, dragons' heads, electric lights, gymnastic rings and trapezes, diving board, poolside changing cubicles and even the hanging baskets of ferns are visible in this atmospheric photograph of the pool hall by Bedford Lemere & Co., taken five months after the official opening on 29 April 1898. The pool was closed in 1986 and the pool hall converted to a gymnasium. At the time of writing, the building is undergoing a £3m refurbishment for use as the town's library.

DOLLAN BATHS, BROUSTER HILL, EAST KILBRIDE, 1960–8

Listed Category A
Photo: RCAHMS

The architect, Alexander Buchanan Campbell, and consulting engineers, T. Harley Haddow & Partners, designed the extraordinary concrete structure of the Dollan Baths in 1966 for the East Kilbride Development Corporation. The Metabolist architecture of Kenzo Tange in Japan, which looked to the biological growth of natural organisms, may have been a subliminal influence on Buchanan Campbell. Four elliptical concrete shells span between pre-stressed concrete arch ribs across the 232-feet width of the building. The £600,000 building was named after Sir Patrick J. Dollan, chairman of the Deveopment Corporation, and was the first Olympic-sized swimming pool in Scotland.

or sometimes bathing cubicles. A number of pools, such as the Western Baths in Glasgow, incorporated hanging gymnastic equipment such as rings and trapezes, and fixed diving platforms, or 'dails', of cast-iron with wooden treads and boards.

Throughout the late nineteenth century and into the early twentieth century, there was continual experimentation with water pumps, heating apparatus, filtering equipment, and disinfection chemicals for swimming pools. Dundee's Corporation Baths initially drew their water directly from the River Tay without heating, filtering or disinfection. The steam-powered centrifugal pumps could fill the large pool in three quarters of an hour and empty it back into the river in twenty minutes.[8] This 'fill and empty' system prevailed as the main way of water cleansing in all the early pools, with cycles every other day for first class pools and sometimes weekly cycles for other pools. Glasgow's first public swimming baths, Greenhead (1878), obtained the 90,625 gallons of water required to fill the men's pool from the new Loch Katrine supply to the city, although it left clay sediment at the bottom.[9] Cleaning and re-filling took three hours and in winter the water could be heated from 50° to 70° Fahrenheit in two hours. Modern recreational pools are usually considerably warmer at 29° Celsius, or 84.2° Fahrenheit. Aeration and filtration through graded sand and gravel was another technology that developed in the late nineteenth century in an

ARLINGTON BATHS CLUB, 61 ARLINGTON STREET, GLASGOW, 1871
Listed Category A

The pool at the Arlington Baths is the oldest surviving private indoor pool in Britain. The Glasgow Swimming Bath Company (Limited) was established in 1870 to construct the baths for £1,700, and a new men-only swimming club formed to lease the baths at 5 per cent of the capital cost per annum. The architect was John Burnet Senior, the father of John James Burnet, who later designed the baths at Drumsheugh in Edinburgh and at Alloa. A novel feature of the Arlington Baths, recorded in the Dundee Advertiser, was that 'by means of the boiler, the large swimming bath will be heated in winter, so that swimming can be practised at any time of the year'. The pool and private baths, which opened in August 1871, were hugely successful, leading to the addition of a Turkish Room with domed roof and exotic coloured glass lights in 1875. Further additions followed in 1893 and 1902. The main top-lit hall retains its 21 m pool and open timber trussed roof with hanging rings and trapezes for gymnastics. Membership is now open to all.

attempt to keep the water clean without frequent flushing and re-filling. 'Scum troughs' around the edge of the water level also helped to remove surface detritus. Often spittoons were provided around the pool, and toilets or urinals placed nearby to discourage pollution of the water.[10] By 1890 needle baths (showering) and footbaths became obligatory before entering most public pools. The baths supplied both clean costumes and towels in order to minimise the introduction of dirt into the water.

By the outbreak of the First World War, there were some twenty-eight public indoor swimming pool establishments throughout Scotland: elevn in Glasgow, five in Edinburgh, two in Dunfermline, and one each in Aberdeen, Leith, Hamilton, Clydebank, Perth, Port Glasgow, Peterhead, Alloa, Forfar and Alva.[11] Although some indoor pools were constructed in the inter-war years, this was the great period of building for outdoor pools. After the First World War there was a great improvement in the technology, which was incorporated into new pools and retro-fitted to some of the earlier pools. Constant circulation of water and the addition of disinfectants became common, as knowledge increased about the role of bacteria and viruses in the spread of disease. Electricity replaced steam-power and gas as the means of pumping water and lighting the baths. The construction of separate female pools ceased and mixed bathing became the norm, although most venues retained some women-only times.

Almost all public pools closed for the duration of the Second World War. There was no money and materials remained scarce after the war, so those pools that re-opened were patched up as best could be afforded. It was the late 1950s before the austerity of the war years began to ease, and the major programme of re-housing the populace of the overcrowded inner cities began in earnest. A number of New Towns were established for the purpose, and it was here that several of the new generation of public pools were constructed as part of the social infrastructure: Dollan Baths at East Kilbride (1960–8, Alexander Buchanan Campbell, and consulting engineers T. Harley Haddow & Partners); Glenrothes (1963–9, William Fraser Pullar, project architect for Fife County Education Architect's Depatment); Cumbernauld (1964–74, Dorward Matheson Gleave & Partners); Irvine (1976, Barry Maitland for Irvine New Town Development Corporation).[12] A swimming pool was planned, but not built in the first phase of Livingston. As curbs on public spending took effect in the 1980s, maintenance of historic pools was squeezed, and many were closed and demolished, or converted to other uses. New buildings of this period favoured leisure pools and complexes, with irregular shapes, wave machines, flumes and other facilities.

OUTDOOR POOLS

The formation of outdoor swimming pools has its roots in the rise of sea- and river-bathing as a fashionable activity for health and beauty from the eighteenth century onwards. In response to the large number of summer drownings, the Humane

STONEHAVEN HEATED OPEN AIR POOL, QUEEN ELIZABETH PARK, STONEHAVEN, 1933–4
Listed Category B

Stonehaven Town Council resolved to build a new 'swimming pool or open bathing place and yachting and paddling pond' on 10 July 1933. Robert Gall of the local firm of architects, Gregory & Gall, designed the 55-yard seawater pool, high diving board and chute, along with the accompanying pavilion and electrically heated changing cubicles, which opened on 2 June

1934. After a councillor's visit to Port Seton pool, the Stonehaven design was reoriented to face west in an attempt to provide more shelter and increased sunshine. The pavilion is long and low, in a traditional style with a pitched red-tiled roof and Art Deco details to the entrance. The construction of the pool was controversial locally, and after much criticism of the first season and the development of a rival facility at Arbroath, a filtration, sterilisation and heating plant was added in 1935. Threatened with closure in the 1990s, the pool is now operated by partnership between the Friends of Stonehaven Pool and Aberdeenshire Council.

Society constructed a rescue house on Glasgow Green overlooking the River Clyde in 1790.[13] Bathing boxes and springboards were later added in the same location. Societies, such as the Forth Swimming Club, instituted at the Newhaven chain pier in 1850, began the promotion of swimming as an organised sporting activity.[14] North Berwick opened its first tidal swimming pool at Milsey Bay Beach in 1840, but it was the coming of the railways in the same decade that really opened up the seaside to mass tourism. Railway travel made trips to the seaside easy and affordable, and many coastal towns vied with each other to provide attractions, including swimming pools. Outdoor pool-building flourished particularly around 1900, for example in Peterhead, where the Corporation built two pools, one indoor and one outdoor, on a rocky embankment beside the sea in 1899.[15] Many other towns, such as St Andrews (Step Rock Pool, 1902 and Ladies' Pool, 1904), built much simpler concrete enclosures for tidal pools.

The cheap transport and increased leisure time of the working population in the 1920s and 1930s saw the heyday of the outdoor pool. Large numbers of tidal pools were constructed at locations all around the Scottish coastline. Towns like

Grangemouth (1930), Macduff (Tarlair, 1935), Prestwick (1931) seeking to enhance their resort status provided more sophisticated lido-type complexes of pools, changing rooms, viewing areas, sunbathing terraces and cafés, often using the latest fashionable Jazz Moderne or Art Deco styles. After complaints in its first operating season, a water heating system was added to the competition-sized Stonehaven Pool in 1935.[16] The magnificent Art Deco pool at Portobello (1936) had the first outdoor artificial wave machine in Britain.[17] Non-coastal (freshwater) pools were relatively rare: an Olympic-sized pool on Glasgow Green was begun in 1939, but abandoned after the war; Carbeth (1933), a weekend retreat of holiday huts in the Campsie Fells, was another example; and the former mining community of New Cumnock (1968) has the only inland outdoor pool still in operation in Scotland. From the 1960s, cheap air travel and package holidays abroad saw the decline and closure of most outdoor pools in Scotland. The remnants of tidal pools remain around the coast, but there are only two operational outdoor seawater pools surviving at Gourock (1909/1935) and Stonehaven (1934), both heated.

Tennis, Rackets and Squash

ROYAL TENNIS COURT, FALKLAND PALACE, EAST PORT, FALKLAND, FIFE, 1539–41

Listed Category A

The Royal Tennis Court of 1539–41 at Falkland Palace is Scotland's earliest surviving work of sporting architecture, and the oldest tennis court still in use anywhere in the world. The master of works records for James V's remodelling of the palace identify the master mason John Brownhill in connection with the tennis court project. The high walls of the court were never roofed, but it had a 'toofall', 'penthouse' or 'pentice' – a lean-to roofed viewing gallery along two sides of the interior. The accounts detail the construction of hazards, which possibly include the four openings ('lunes') in the back wall. The interior walls appear to have been painted black. Although the adjoining late sixteenth-century structure has been used as stables/byre, it is possible that it was used originally for games such as billiards or bowling. John Kinross restored the tennis court for the 3rd Marquess of Bute in 1892–94, Walter Schomberg Scott repaired it for the National Trust for Scotland in 1955, and repairs were carried out in 2010–11.

While its roots are firmly planted in twelfth-century France, tennis is very much a part of Scottish history and Scotland can claim to have the oldest tennis court in the world, the Royal Tennis Court at Falkland Palace.

The Official Gateway to Scotland

ROYAL OR REAL TENNIS

The term 'real tennis' was adopted in the twentieth century to distinguish the ancient royal game played in an enclosed court from modern lawn tennis. In the late fifteenth and sixteenth centuries, the game was known as 'caiche', 'caitche' or 'cache' and the tennis court as a 'cachepell' in Scotland. In the 1599 Edinburgh edition of his book of instruction to his son Henry, 'Basilikon Doron', James VI used the term 'caitche', but added 'tennise' in the 1603 London edition.[1] At this period the game was played in a high-walled court with the roofs of either two or three lean-to galleries forming part of the playing area. In some cases the ball was struck with a racket, but often the hand was used. The sport-loving monarchs James IV, James V and James VI constructed such courts in the sixteenth century at the royal residences of Holyroodhouse, Stirling Palace, Dunfermline Palace, Linlithgow Palace and Falkland Palace, and at royal lodgings in Perth and Aberdeen.[2] When preparations were in train for James VI's visit to Scotland in 1617, the bailies of Edinburgh and Leith were instructed to put the tennis courts in order.[3] Although 'royal tennis' was the sport of kings, wealthy patrons built private courts in the larger burghs, including Stirling and Edinburgh, and at private houses in the country. In spite of not being a great sports enthusiast himself, Gavin Hamilton, 7th Laird of Raploch, Larkhall, South Lanarkshire, built a new house in the late sixteenth century with a courtyard to the dimensions of a tennis court so that guests could play there.[4] It is likely that such yards were common. The only surviving ancient royal tennis court building is at Falkland Palace, but indoor courts were still being built in the late eighteenth century, for

EGLINTON CASTLE RACKETS HALL, EGLINTON COUNTRY PARK, NORTH AYRSHIRE, ABOUT 1840
Listed Category B

Built by Archibald Montgomerie, 13th Earl of Eglinton, in the 1840s, the hall at Eglinton Castle is the oldest surviving rackets court in the world, and the oldest purpose-built indoor sports venue in Scotland. The mason responsible is possibly David Andrew, but the architect and precise date of construction have yet to be indentified. Externally the court borrows the form of a chapel with a pedimented classical front, but there are no side windows and the building is top-lit by strips of glazing in the roof. The main feature of the interior is the timber kingpost roof. A modern timber floor now covers the large granite slabs of the playing surface. Originally the entrance provided stair access to a viewing gallery. The hall is now used as an events and exhibition space.

example the subscription court at Mitchell Street in Glasgow.[5] The architect Joseph Bickley of Fryers & Penman constructed a new court for the Paisley thread manufacturer and real tennis enthusiast, J.O.M. Clark, at his Troon villa as late as 1905.

TENNIS, RACKETS AND SQUASH

The credit for the invention of the modern game of lawn tennis is disputed. Some historians attribute the game to the experiments of Thomas Henry Gem and Augurio Perera at Edgbaston, England, in 1859, while others champion Walter Clopton Wingfield, who patented his portable 'Sphairistikè' or 'Lawn Tennis' court in 1874. Lawn tennis was first played in Scotland in 1875, and quickly gained in popularity. Its success was due to it being a very contained and sociable game, the relatively small amount of space and equipment required, and the fact that it could be played easily on any relatively flat surface. By the 1880s, many newly-established croquet lawns were converted to host lawn tennis. Like croquet, tennis was played by women from the outset, and mixed games of doubles were an early feature of the sport. As with other lawn sports, pavilions were essential for shelter, changing and toilet facilities. Frequently early pavilions were built to service both tennis and bowling clubs. One of the earliest joint pavilions was constructed for the Titwood Bowling and Tennis Club in Glasgow in 1890, but as the tennis section grew, a new pavilion for tennis was designed in a modest Baroque form by Robert James Walker in 1913 (completed 1925).[6]

In the late eighteenth century the sport of rackets (alternatively known as 'racquets', 'racquet' or 'racket') is supposed to have developed from a debtors' prison recreation in London, where it was taken up by a number of schools and the rules were codified. Squash was invented at Harrow School in about 1830, when pupils found that a punctured rackets ball 'squashed' on impact with the wall, and made for a faster and more varied game. The first dedicated rackets courts were built at the school in 1850 and squash courts followed in 1864. The two sports continued in parallel. Only rackets was taken up at an early date in Scotland, and it was the 1920s before squash became popular. Rackets was, like many sports of the period, considered 'manly', and 'by exercising every joint and member of the body, furnishes one of the most healthful and exhilarating of gymnastic employments'.[7] The extravagant 13th Earl of Eglinton built his own rackets court at Eglinton Castle near Irvine in the early 1840s, followed by another court in Dublin during one of his two periods as viceroy, and inaugurated a rackets club at 285 Bath Street, Glasgow, in 1860, designed by John Thomas Rochead and constructed at a cost of £3,000. There was a similar facility at 180 Rose Street, Edinburgh, where Prince Alfred gained a black eye playing the sport in February 1864.[8] Another Rose Street player, Herbert Lawford, went on to become the men's singles tennis champion at Wimbledon in 1887.[9]

By the time the Scottish Squash Raquets Association and the Scottish Women's Squash Raquets Association formed respectively in 1936 and 1937, there were courts in Edinburgh at Bell's Mills, Malloch Street in Glasgow and in Aberdeen. There were also courts at three private schools: George Watson's College, Edinburgh Academy and Fettes College, and numerous private houses.[10]

Scotland Rugby Team by
unknown photographer, 1877
National Galleries of Scotland,
Edinburgh

Notes

SCOTLAND'S SPORTING HISTORY · PAGES 9–23

1. Callander 2003, pp.19–20 outlines the history of 'burgh commons'.

2. See Jamieson 1994, p.31 for accounts of archery butts at Holyroodhouse and tennis courts at Stirling, Falkland, Linlithgow and Holyrood.

3. Dunbar 1999, pp.202–4.

4. Dunbar 1999, pp.205–8.

5. Morley 1888, p.155.

6. Rodger 1992, p.405.

7. David Wedderburn, *Vocabula cum aliis nonnullis Latinæ linguæ subsidiis*, written in 1636; Glasgow, 1691 edition via Special Collections, University of Glasgow.

8. Geddes 2007, pp.18–20, pp.96–98. Irons 1898, vol.2, p.402. Burnett 2000, p.68.

9. Somerville 1815, vol.I, pp.140–1.

10. See the index and illustrations to Brown 2012 for numerous examples of bowling greens attached to country houses.

11. Strathmore 1890, p.44.

12. Geddes 2007, p.33.

13. McLellan 1894, pp.26–7.

14. Stark 1825, p.270.

15. Chambers 1838, vol.I, p.382.

16. Manson 1919, p.142.

17. Perris 2008, pp.20–5.

18. Burnett 2000, p.43.

19. 'Toxophilite' is derived from the Ancient Greek words τοξον and φιλος, meaning 'bow' and 'love', which were put together in 1535 by Roger Ascham to form the title of his book, *Toxophilus*, or 'lover of the bow'. Many archery societies adopt the word in their names.

20. *Inverness Courier*, 6 December 1849, p.3.

21. Academical 1954.

22. Tranter 1989, p.240.

23. O'Brien 2010, p.18.

24. McLellan 1894, p.18, p.41.

25. McLellan 1894, p.43.

26. McLellan 1894, p.19.

27. McLellan 1894, p.139 (in relation to Elder Park in 1885, where Mrs Elder's gift of the park was dependent on a ban on cricket and football).

28. These random examples are drawn from Burnett 2000, Jackson 1998 and Tranter 1989.

29. *Caledonian Mercury*, 23 December 1859, p.1.

30. Appleton 2009.

31. Bilsborough 1983, pp.78–9.

32. Jarvie & Burnett 2000, pp.25–6.

33. Keddie 1983, p.1.

34. St Leonards School website: www.stleonards-fife.org.

35. Smith 1981, plates 5 and 6, and pp.158–62.

36. *Evening Telegraph*, 26 July 1937, p.8.

37. Perris 2008, p.34.

38. *Ayrshire Post*, 5 May 1961, p.10. The article notes the influence of television on the town council's decision to provide the new sports arena at Dam Park in Ayr.

39. Inglis 2005 A, p.1998; Inglis 1996, p.423.

ARCHERY · PAGES 24–27

1. Balfour Paul 1875, p.62.

2. Act of Parliament, Perth, 26 May 1424.

3. Balfour Paul 1894, p.235.

4. Adamson 1620, p.21 (note).

5. Balfour Paul 1894, p.239.

6. Balfour Paul 1875, p.15 states that 'in recent days ladies' clubs have become quite an institution'.

BOWLING AND SKITTLES · PAGES 28–35

1. Somerville 1861, pp.345–6.

2. See Burnett 2000, pp.31–45.

3. Accounts 1877–1978, vol.1, p.332.

4. Marwick 1869–92, vol.4, p.214 (4 August 1581).

5. Adamson 1620, p.5.

6. Dunbar 1999, p.205.

7. Omond 1887, p.45 (plan), p.49.

8. East Lothian Council Archive Service, ref. HAD/2/1/2/6.

9. Allen 1844, p.450.

10. Munro 1899, vol.1, pp.150–1.

11. Marwick And Renwick 1876–1916, vol. iv, p.158 [13 April 1695].

12. The bowling green at Cowane's Hospital was completed on 31 August 1713, as recorded in the Hospital's minutes. George Heriot's Hospital laid out two greens in 1768.

13. Perris 2008, pp.20–2.

14. Anonymous 1818, p.193.

15. Dalgleish 1990, pp.189–200.

16. Armet 1956, pp.185–7.

17. Burnett 2000, p.45.

18. Brown 1892, pp.10–11.

19. Inglis 2005/B, pp.24–5.

20. O'Brien 2010, pp.38–9.

21. O'Brien 2010, p.156.

CRICKET · PAGES 36–41

1. *The Pump*, written under the pseudonym 'Bailzie Peakodde', relates the story of Bob Maxwell, the hero of the Glasgow side,

who was tricked to prevent him appearing in a match against Perth. The impatient crowd of 'squire, commoner and whore', waiting on Glasgow Green, shower 'a cloud of dogs and cats' at the home team, and are about 'to brain them with their bats' when Bob arrives on a stretcher. He relates how he has been imprisoned by Squire Thomson, and set the impossible task of pumping up water into an unplugged bath to obtain his release.

2. Penman 1992.

3. *Morning Post*, 22 January 1778.

4. *The Scottish Antiquary* vol.11, Edinburgh 1897, p.82. See also National Records for Scotland, National Register of Archives for Scotland: ref. NRAS332/F/1/1028, accounts for 8th Duke of Hamilton's cricket expenses, 1782; ref. NRAS2177/ bundle 5350, subscription to Thomas Lord and note of £10 10s 0d paid in cash to unnamed cricket players from 12 July to 10 August 1791.

5. *Caledonian Mercury*, 5 October 1785, p.3.

6. National Library of Scotland Manuscripts Collection, ref. MS.3630. Diary of Mary Graham, entries for 21 July, 6, 20, 22 and 27 August 1785.

7. Reid 1856, vol.3, p.426.

8. Kaczynski 2007, p.4; *Caledonian Mercury* 10 May 1849, p.3.

9. A single storey building, possibly a pavilion, is shown on the Ordnance Survey Town Plan of 1849.

10. Academical 1954, pp.24–5.

11. Burnett 2000, p.253.

12. Bone 1890, p.71.

CURLING · PAGES 42–47

1. Statistical 1834–45, vol.4, Wigtonshire, Inch Parish, 1839, p.89.

2. Kerr 1890, p.30. Kerr points out that the lettering might have been added at a later date.

3. Dalyell 1924, p.357 (In the Saddlehouse).

4. Adamson 1638, p.5.

5. Moncrieff 1990.

6. Brown 2012, pp.322–5.

7. Kerr 1890, p.115.

8. Macdonald 1899, p.197.

9. Kerr 1890, p.150.

10. Cairnie 1833.

11. Kerr 1890, p.357.

12. Historical Curling Places: www.historicalcurlingplaces.org.

13. Statistical 1834–45, vol.3, Selkirkshire, Galashiels, p.19.

14. Vamplew 2005, p.265.

FOOTBALL · PAGES 48–57

1. Records of the Parliaments of Scotland to 1707, ref. 1424/19 at www.rps.ac.uk.

2. Accounts 1877–1978, vol.1, p.331.

3. See www.medievalists.net (18 October 2011), Maclean 2013 and Wedderburn 1636.

4. Stark 1806, p.388.

5. Wilkes 1819, p.406.

6. National Records of Scotland, ref. GD253/183/14/12.

7. National Records of Scotland, ref. GD253/183/7/3.

8. Murray 1927, pp.442–5.

9. Robinson 1920, chapter II.

10. Dundee Courier and Argus, 21 May 1873, p.3.

11. Dundee Courier and Argus, 23 March 1874, p.4.

12. All-time Scottish Football Club Directory at www.scottish-football-historical-archive.com.

13. See O'Brien 2010, pp.34–57 for a history of various sporting venues in and around Queen's Park.

14. Glasgow Post Office Directory 1874–5, p.337.

15. Robinson 1920, chapter XXXIII.

16. *Dundee Courier*, 5 November 1878, p.5.

17. Vamplew 1982, p.552.

18. Robinson 1920, chapter XXXIV.

19. Robinson 1920, chapters XLII and LXII.

20. *The Illustrated Sporting and Dramatic News*, 2 June 1888 (lithograph).

21. *Glasgow Herald*, 9 April 1894, p.9.

22. *Dundee Courier*, 2 November, 1899, p.2 (quotation); *Edinburgh Evening News*, 27 October 1899, p.5; O'Brien 2010, p.67.

23. Inglis 2005 A.

24. Shiels 1998, pp.148–55.

25. Robinson 1920, chapter XXXV.

26. Inglis 2005 A, p.175.

GOLF · PAGES 58–65

1. RPS 2007–12, Act Anent Wapinschawingis (Edinburgh, 7 March 1458), at www.rps.ac.uk.

2. Accounts 1877–1987, vol.2

3. Geddes 2007, pp.23–70.

4. Clark 1893, p.109.

5. National Library of Scotland, ref. Acc. 11208/2. Geddes 2007, pp.87–94 and pp.98–100.

6. For the Golf House at the eastern end of Bruntsfield Links (modernday corner of Meadows Place and Roseneath Place) see National Library of Scotland, ref. EMS.S.632, *A plan of the city and suburbs of Edinburgh* by Alexander Kincaid, published 1784.

7. National Library of Scotland, ref. Acc. 11208/3, Sederunt Book for the Subscribers for Building the Golf House, 23 April 1768 – 27 November 1779, and ref. Acc. 11208/85, papers regarding the sale of the Golf House 1833–6. *Caledonian Mercury*, 16 February 1780, p.1. RCAHMS, ref. DP 161895, National Art Survey, plans of Leith Links Old Golf House. Grant 1865, vol.VI, p.262, Paton 1877, pp.210–11, Clark 1893, p.47, Irons 1898, pp.408–9.

8. National Records of Scotland, ref. GD113/4/158/241, letter of January 1788 from William Grant in London to Gilbert Innes of Stow stating that he understands golf to be the fashionable amusement in Edinburgh.

9. Baxter 1899, pp.101–2.

10. *New York Times*, 26 April 1904.

11. See Bauchope 1889 for a list of golf clubs and their home greens.

12. See the 'Early History of the Club' and 'The Royal & Ancient Clubhouse' in the 'Our Heritage' section of the R & A website: www.randa.org.

13. Clark 1893, p.40, p.88, pp.108–9.

14. See the 'History' section of the Kilsyth Lennox Golf Club website: www.kilsythlennox.com.

15. Geddes 2007, pp.15–16.

16. Clark 1898, p.91.

17. Dictionary of Scottish Architects: www.scottisharchitects.org.uk [building name

search on 'Ladies Golf'; accessed 12 February 2014]. *Dundee Courier*, 19 April 1897, p.6 (Lundin Links).

18. RCAHMS, ref. DPM 1900/120/1, plans, sections and elevations of Cramond Brig Golf Club by Murphy & Kinross, 1908.

HIGHLAND GAMES & ATHLETICS · PAGES 66–71

1. Ceres Highland Games website history section: www.ceresgames.co.uk.

2. Webster 1973, p.11.

3. Buildings of Scotland: Perth & Kinross, p.685.

4. See the history section of the St Ronan's Border Games website: www.stronansgames.org.

5. Keddie 1982, p.1.

6. Keddie 1982, p.3.

7. *Dundee Courier*, 30 December 1869, p.3.

8. Keddie 1982, p.14.

HORSE-RACING · PAGES 72–77

1. Accounts 1877–1978, vol.2, p.428.

2. Burnett 1998, p.56, pp.68–71.

3. Burnett 1998, pp.59–62.

4. For example at Dumfries, described in McDowall 1867, p.359.

5. Haig 1825, pp.135–6.

6. RCAHMS, ref. DP161894, 'Plan of Leith Sands compared with the Meadows and Burntfield Links' by Thomas Bonnar, 16 November 1811.

7. *Caledonian Mercury*, 11 October 1819, p.3 and 16 October 1819, p.3.

8. National Records of Scotland, ref. GD3/3/203, miscellaneous

vouchers, including new race course at Bogside.

9. Vamplew 2003, pp.94–111.

10. Close And Riches 2012, p.153.

11. Elspeth King, 'Suffragette Mystery Solved' (8 March 2003) at www.bbc.co.uk/news.

12. *Dundee Courier*, 20 May 1913, p.5.

13. Possibly by J. & J.A. Carrick. See Dictionary of Scottish Architects: www.scottisharchitects.org.uk (search under 'Carrick'; accessed 22 January 2014).

14. See Dictionary of Scottish Architects www.scottisharchitects.org.uk (search under 'Oswald'; accessed 22 January 2014).

ICE SKATING AND ICE HOCKEY · PAGES 78–83

1. Elliot 1971, pp.96–7.

2. Elliot 1971, p.100.

3. Baird 1898, p.266.

4. Murray 1927, p.439.

5. *John O'Groat Journal*, 11 February 1848, p.2.

6. *Glasgow Herald*, 11 October 1895, p.4 and 6 July 1896, p.6.

7. David B. Smith, *Glasgow Real Ice Skating Palace* at www.curlinghistory.blogspot.co.uk (25 April 2010).

8. See www.scottisharchitects.org.uk (search under 'Panorama'; accessed 2 December 2013).

9. O'Brien 2010, pp.168–71.

10. Stirling Local History Society website (Stirling's History/Stirling's Sports/Roller Skating Rink): www.stirling-lhs.org (accessed 2 December 2013).

11. *The Scotsman*, 30 July 1908, p.1.

RUGBY · PAGES 84–87

1. *Glasgow Herald*, 4 March 1873, p.5.

2. Edinburgh Academicals website (Club/History/Historic Timelines): www.edinburghaccies.com (accessed 2 December 2013).

3. *Caledonian Mercury*, 19 January 1858, p.2; *Glasgow Herald*, 26 October 1957, p.4.

4. *Scotsman*, 17 March 1873, p.6.

5. Inglis 2005 B, pp.20–1.

SWIMMING AND AQUATIC SPORTS · PAGES 88–95

1. Campbell 1918, p.66.

2. Campbell 1918, pp.4–5.

3. Glasgow Corporation 1904, p.93.

4. Norrie 1876, pp.23–5.

5. See the website of the Western Baths, Glasgow, for information about early subscribers and clientele: www.thewesternbaths.co.uk/history.

6. Edinburgh Evening News, 19 November 1887, p.3; Dundee Courier & Argus, 26 March 1889, p.4.

7. Campbell 1918, p.107.

8. Norrie 1876, p.24.

9. *Glasgow Herald*, 20 August 1878, p.3.

10. Campbell 1918, pp.97–8.

11. Campbell 1918, p.62.

12. Dictionary of Scottish Architects: www.scottisharchitects.org.uk (building name searches on 'swimming' and 'Magnum'; accessed 12 February 2014).

13. McLellan 1894, pp.36–7.

14. Oliver & Boyd 1857, p.736.

15. *Aberdeen Journal*, 20 June 1899, p.4. The architect is

identified as Mr Anderson of London, and the builders, William Stuart & Son.

16. *Aberdeen Journal*, 5 February 1935, p.5.

17. *Dundee Courier*, 3 May 1935, p.10.

TENNIS, RACKETS AND SQUASH · PAGES 96–98

1. Butler 1887, p.144 (reprint of 1599 edition); Morley 1888, p.155 (reprint of 1603 edition).

2. Jamieson 1994, p.31; Dunbar 1999, pp.205–9.

3. McNeill And McNeill 1996, p.39.

4. Somerville 1815, vol.2, pp.140–1.

5. Reid 1856, vol.3, pp.426–7.

6. O'Brien 2010, pp.88–9.

7. *Glasgow Herald*, 25 September 1860, p.4.

8. *North London News*, 30 April 1864, p.2.

9. Scottish Sport History blog by Andy Mitchell: www.scottish-sporthistory.com.

10. RCAHMS: www.rcahms.gov.uk (search on 'racket'); Dictionary of Scottish Architects: www.scottisharchitects.org.uk (search on 'racket' and 'racquet') and 'History of Scottish Squash' at www.scottishsquash.org (accessed 10 January 2014).

Mr Laing by D.O. Hill and Robert Adamson, 1843
National Galleries of Scotland, Edinburgh

Select Bibliography

ACADEMICAL 1954
Edinburgh Academical Club, *One Hundred Years at Raeburn Place, 1854–1954*, Edinburgh, 1954

ACCOUNTS 1877–1978
Thomas Dickson, (eds) James Balfour Paul et al., *Accounts of the Lord High Treasurer of Scotland*, 13 vols, Edinburgh, 1877–1978

ADAMSON 1620
Henry Adamson (ed. James Cant), *The Muses Threnodie; or Mirthful Mournings on the Death of Mr Gall*, written 1620, published posthumously Edinburgh, 1638, reprinted with introduction, Perth, 1774

ALLEN 1844
James Allen, *The Lamp of Lothian, or, the History of Haddington*, Haddington, 1844

ANONYMOUS 1818
Anonymous, *The New Picture of Edinburgh for 1818, Being a Correct Guide to the Curiosities, Amusements, Public Establishments, and Remarkable Objects In and Near Edinburgh*, Edinburgh, 1818

ANONYMOUS 1828
Anonymous, *The Kilmarnock Treatise on Curling*, Kilmarnock, 1828

ANONYMOUS 1896
Anonymous, 'The Golf-Ball Makers of Leith' in *The Scottish Antiquary, or, Northern Notes and Queries*, vol.10, no.39, Edinburgh, 1896, pp.102–3

ANONYMOUS 1965
Anonymous, 'Variations on a Triangle – A Football Stand at Galashiels' in *Concrete Quarterly* no.66, London, 1965

ANONYMOUS 1966
Anonymous, 'Arched Shells in Lanarkshire' in *Concrete Quarterly*, no.70, London, 1966, pp.5–7

APPLETON 2009
David Appleton, *The History of the Scottish Croquet Championship, 1870–1914*, Newcastle-upon-Tyne, 2009; updated edition available at www.scottishcroquet.org.uk.

ARMET 1956
Helen Armet, 'The Society of Bowlers' in *The Book of the Old Edinburgh Club*, vol. 29, Edinburgh, 1956, pp.185–7

ATKINS 1872
John Ringwood Atkins, *The Book of Racquets: A Practical Guide to the Game and its History, and to the Different Courts in which it is Played*, London, 1872

BAIRD 1898
William Baird, *Annals of Duddingston and Portobello*, Edinburgh, 1898

BALFOUR PAUL 1875
Sir James Balfour Paul, *The History of the Royal Company of Archers: The Queen's Body-Guard for Scotland*, Edinburgh, 1875

BALFOUR PAUL 1894
Sir James Balfour Paul, 'Scottish Archery' in *The Badminton Library of Sports & Pastimes: Archery*, London, 1894, pp.234–47

BAUCHOPE 1889
John Bauchope (ed.), *The Golfing Annual 1888–89*, vol.2, London, 1889; vol.2 of periodical series published annually 1888–1910

BAXTER 1899
Peter Baxter, *Golf in Perth and Perthshire: Traditional, Historical, and Modern*, Perth, 1899

BILSBOROUGH 1983
Peter Bilsborough, *The Development of Sport in Glasgow, 1850–1914* (M.Litt. Thesis for the University of Stirling, June 1983); available at the Stirling Online Research Repository: www.dspace.stir.ac.uk.

BLAINE 1870
Delabere P. Blaine, *An Encyclopaedia of Rural Sports*, London, 1870

BOLSOVER 1959
Godfrey R. Bolsover, *Who's Who and Encyclopaedia of Bowls*, Nottingham, 1959

BONE 1890
David Bone, *Scottish Football Reminiscences and Sketches*, Glasgow, 1890

BONE 1898
David Bone, *Fifty Years Reminiscences of Scottish Cricket*, Glasgow, 1898

BROOK 1891
Alexander J.S. Brook, 'Notice of the Silver Bell of Lanark, a Horse-Racing Trophy of the Seventeenth Century, with Some References to the Early Practice of Horse-Racing in Scotland' in *Proceedings of the Society of Antiquaries of Scotland*, vol.25, Edinburgh, pp.174–88

BROWN 1892
James Brown, *Manual of Bowling*, Edinburgh, 1892

BROWN 2012
Marilyn Brown, *Scotland's Lost Gardens*, Edinburgh, 2012

BUILDINGS OF SCOTLAND SERIES
(various authors and dates)

BURMAN 2008
Peter Burman, *Archers' Hall Conservation Statement*, Edinburgh, 2008

BURNETT 1998
John Burnett, 'The Sites and Landscapes of Horse Racing in Scotland before 1860' in *The Sports Historian*, no.18, Manchester, 1998, pp.55–75

BURNETT 2000
John Burnett, *Riot, Revelry and Rout: Sport in Lowland Scotland Before 1860*, East Linton, 2000

BURNETT 2005
John Burnett, 'Sports in the Countryside' and 'Sport in Scotland' in *Scottish Life and Society: The Individual and Community Life*, East Linton, 2005

BUTLER 1887
Charles Butler (ed.), *Basilikon Doron, or His Majestys Instructions to his Dearest Sonne, Henry the Prince*, written by James VI and I, Edinburgh, 1599, reprinted for the Roxburghe Club, London, 1887

BUTLER AND WORDIE 1989
Lance St John Butler and P.J. Wordie, *The Royal Game*, Kippen, 1989

CAIRNIE 1833
John Cairnie, *Essay on Curling and Artificial Pond Making*, Glasgow, 1833

CALLANDER 2003
Robin Callander, *The History of Common Land in Scotland*, 2003; available at www.scottish-commons.org.

CAMPBELL 1918
Agnes Campbell, *Report on Public Baths and Wash-houses in the United Kingdom*, London, 1918

CAMPBELL 1993
Douglas Campbell, *Scottish Baths 1868–1914 and their Conservation* (unpublished MSc dissertation, Heriot-Watt University, 1993)

CHAMBERS 1838
Robert and William Chambers, *Gazetteer of Scotland*, 2 vols, Glasgow, 1838

CLARK 1893
Robert Clark (ed.), *Golf: A Royal & Ancient Game*, London and New York, 1893

CLOSE AND RICHES 2012
Rob Close and Anne Riches, *The Buildings of Scotland: Ayrshire and Arran*, New Haven and London, 2012

COX 1991
Richard William Cox, *Sport in Britain – A Bibliography of Historical Publications*, Manchester, 1991

CRUFT, DUNBAR AND FAWCETT 2006
Kitty Cruft, John Dunbar and Richard Fawcett, *The Buildings of Scotland: Borders*, New Haven and London, 2006

DALGLEISH 1990
George R. Dalgleish, 'The "Silver Jack" Trophy of the Edinburgh Society of Bowlers' in *Proceedings of the Society of Antiquaries of Scotland*, vol.120, Edinburgh, 1990, pp.189–200

DALYELL 1924
James Dalyell (ed.), 'Inventory of the Plenishing of the House of the Binns at the Date of the Death of General Thomas Dalyell, 21st August 1685' in *Proceedings of the Society of Antiquities of Scotland*, vol.58, Edinburgh, 1924, pp.344–70

DARVILL 1838
Richard Darvill, *A Treatise on the Care, Treatment, and Training of the English Race Horse*, London, 1838

DUNBAR 1999
John G. Dunbar, *Scottish Royal Palaces: the Architecture of the Royal Residences in the Late Medieval and Early Renaissance Periods*, East Linton, 1999

ELLIOT 1971
Margaret Elliot, 'The Edinburgh Skating club' in *The Book of the Old Edinburgh Club*, vol. xxxiii, part 2, Edinburgh, 1971, pp.96–136

EVERARD 1907
Harry Stirling Crawfurd Everard, *History of The Royal & Ancient Golf Club, St Andrews, from 1754–1900*, Edinburgh and London, 1907

FAIRFAX-BLAKEBOROUGH 1973
John Fairfax-Blakeborough, *Northern Turf History*, vol.iv, Westerdale, 1973

FITTIS 1891
Robert Scott Fittis, *Sports and Pastimes of Scotland*, Paisley, 1891

FLANNERY 2004
Michael Flannery and Richard Leech, *Golf Through The Ages, 600 Years of Golfing Art*, Fairfield, Iowa, 2004

FLEMING 1919
David Hay Fleming, 'The Accounts of Dr Alexander Skene, Provost of St Salcator's College, St Andrews, Relating to the Extensive Repairs of the College Buildings, the Church, and the Steeple, 1683–1690' in *Proceedings of the Society of Antiquaries of Scotland*, vol.54, Edinburgh, 1920, pp.216–48

GEDDES 2007
Olive M. Geddes, *A Swing Through Time: Golf in Scotland 1457–1744*, Edinburgh, 2007

GEORGE 1997
Jane George, 'Women and Golf in Scotland' in *Oral History*, vol.25, no.I, London, 1997

GILLMEISTER 1997
Heiner Gillmeister, *Tennis: A Cultural History*, London, 1997

GLASGOW CORPORATION 1904
Glasgow Corporation, *Souvenir Handbook of Glasgow, issued by the Corporation on the occasion of the Twenty-Second Congress of The Sanitary Institute held in Glasgow from 25th till 30th July, 1904*, Glasgow, 1904

GLENDINNING 1997
John Richards, 'The Architecture of Precision: the Royal Commonwealth Pool' in Miles Glendinning (ed.), *Rebuilding Scotland: the Postwar Vision 1945–75*, East Linton, 1997, pp.125–9

GORDON AND INGLIS 2009
Ian Gordon and Simon Inglis, *Great Lengths*, London, 2009

GRANT 1865
James Grant, *Old and New Edinburgh*, 6 vols, Edinburgh, 1865

HAIG 1825
James Haig, *A Topographical and Historical Account of the Town of Kelso, and of the Town and Castle of Roxburgh*, Edinburgh, 1825

HAMILTON 1998
David Hamilton, *Golf: Scotland's Game*, Kilmacolm, 1998

HARRIS 2005
Martin C. Harris, *Homes of British Ice Hockey*, Stroud, 2005

HORNBY 2008
Hugh Hornby, *Uppies and Downies – The Extraordinary Football Games of Britain*, London, 2008

HORNBY 2014
Hugh Hornby, *Bowled Over – The Bowling Greens of Britain*, London, 2014

HUTCHINSON 1897
Horace Hutchinson (ed.), *British Golf Links*, London, 1897

INGLIS 1996
Simon Inglis, *Football Grounds of Britain* (3rd edition), London, 1996

INGLIS 2005 A
Simon Inglis, *Engineering Archie: Archibald Leitch – Football Ground Designer*, London, April 2005

INGLIS 2005 B
Simon Inglis, *A Load of Old Balls*, London, October 2005

IRONS 1898
James Campbell Irons, *Leith and its Antiquities from the Earliest Times to the Close of the Nineteenth Century*, 2 vols, Edinburgh, 1898

JACKSON 1998
Lorna Jackson, 'Sport and Patronage: Evidnce from Nineteenth Century Argyllshire' in the *Sports Historian*, vol.18, no.2, November 1998

JAMIESON 1994
Fiona Jamieson, 'The Royal Gardens of the Palace of Holyroodhouse, 1500–1603' in *Garden History*, vol. 22, no. 1, London, 1994, pp.18–36

JARVIE AND BURNETT 2000
Grant Jarvie and John Burnett (eds.), *Sport, Scotland and the Scots*, East Linton, 2000

JONES 1772
Robert Jones, *A Treatise on Skating*, London, 1772

KACZYNSKI 2007
Brian Kaczynski, *Grange Cricket Club 175*, Edinburgh, 2007

KEDDIE 1982
John W. Keddie, *Scottish Athletics, 1883–1983: the Official Centenary Publication of the Scottish Amateur Athletic Association*, Edinburgh, 1982

KERR 1890
John Kerr, *A History of Curling*, Edinburgh, 1890

MACCALLUM 2004
Malcolm MacCallum, 'Swimming in Scotland in the first half of the twentieth century' in *Review of Scottish Culture*, vol.16, Edinburgh, 2003–4

MACDONALD 1899
John A.R. MacDonald, *The History of Blairgowrie*, Blairgowrie, 1899

MACLEAN 2013
Robert MacLean, 'More than a Game: How Scotland Shaped World Football' University of Glasgow Library Special Collections blog at www.universityofglasgowlibrary.wordpress.com (Glasgow, 5 April 2013)

MANSON 1919
James Alexander Manson, *The Complete Bowler: Being the History and Practice of the Ancient and Royal Game of Bowls*, London, 1919

MARWICK 1869–92
James David Marwick (ed.), *Extracts from the Records of the Burgh of Edinburgh*, 5 vols, Edinburgh, 1869–82

MARWICK AND RENWICK 1876–1916
James David Marwick and Robert Renwick, *Extracts from the Records of the Burgh of Glasgow, A.D. 1573–1717*, 4 vols, Glasgow, 1876–1916

MASSIE 1984
Alan Massie, *A Portrait of Scottish Rugby*, Edinburgh, 1984

McDOWALL 1867
William McDowall, *History of the Burgh of Dumfries*, Edinburgh, 1867

McKEAN 1987
Charles McKean, *The Scottish Thirties: An Architectural Introduction*, Edinburgh, 1987

McKEAN 2004
Charles McKean, 'Buildings for Recreation' in *Scottish Life and Society: Scotland's Buildings*, East Linton, 2004

McNEILL AND McNEILL 1996
William A. McNeill and Peter G.B. McNeill, 'The Scottish Progress of James VI, 1617' in *The Scottish Historical Review*, vol.lxxv, no.199, part 1, Edinburgh, 1996, pp.38–51

MITCHELL 1864
William Wallace Mitchell, *Manual of Bowl-Playing; Containing Laws and Rules of the Game, and Hints to Directors and Players, Etc.*, Glasgow, 1864

McLELLAN 1894
Duncan McLellan, *Glasgow Public Parks*, Glasgow, 1894

MONCRIEFF 1990
Rhoderick and Alison Moncrieff (eds), *The Annals of Kinross-shire*, Kinross, 1990

MORLEY 1888
Henry Morley (ed.), *A Miscellany containing The Basilikon Doron of King James I...*, London, 1888

MUNRO 1899
Alexander MacDonald Munro (ed.), *Records of Old Aberdeen*, 2 vols, Aberdeen, 1899

MURRAY 1927
David Murray, *Memories of the Old College of Glasgow*, Glasgow, 1927

NORRIE 1876
William Norrie, *Penny Handbook to the Public Institutions of Dundee*, Dundee, 1876; available at www.scran.ac.uk

O'BRIEN 2010
Ged O'Brien, *Played in Glasgow*, London, 2010

OLIVER AND BOYD 1857
Oliver and Boyd's New Edinburgh Almanac and National Repository for the Year 1857, Edinburgh, 1857

OMOND 1887
George W.T. Omond, *The Arniston Memoirs: Three Centuries of a Scottish House, 1571–1838*, Edinburgh, 1887

PARKER 2001
Claire Parker, 'The Rise of Competitive Swimming 1840 to 1878' in *The Sports Historian*, vol.21, no.2, 2001

PATON 1877
Hugh Paton, *A series of original portraits and caricature etchings by the late John Kay. With biographical sketches and illustrative anecdotes*, 2 vols, Edinburgh, 1837, revised edition, 1877

PEARSON 2011
Lynn Pearson, *The Architecture of Cricket Pavilions: Home and Away*, Newcastle-upon-Tyne, 2011; available at www.academia.eu

PENMAN 1992
Richard Penman, 'The Failure of Cricket in Scotland' in *International Journal for the History of Sport*, vol.9, no 2, London, 1992, pp.302–15

PERRIS 2008
Jeff Perris, *All About Bowls – The History, Construction and Maintenance of Bowling Greens*, Bingley, 1988, 3rd edition, 2008

POTTER 1999
David W. Potter, *The Encyclopedia of Scottish Cricket*, Manchester, 1999

PRETSELL 1908
James M. Pretsell, *The Game of Bowls – Past and Present*, Edinburgh, 1908

REID 1856
Robert Reid, *Glasgow Past and Present*, 3 vols, Glasgow, 1856

ROBERTSON 1995
George Robertson, *Tennis in Scotland: 100 years of the Scottish Lawn Tennis Association 1895–1995*, Edinburgh, 1995

ROBINSON 1920
Richard Robinson, *History of the Queen's Park Football Club 1867–1917*, Glasgow, 1920

RODGER 1992
Robin H. Rodger, 'The Silver Ball of Rattray: a Unique Sporting Trophy' in *Proceedings of the Society of Antiquaries of Scotland*, vol.122, Edinburgh, 1992, pp.403–11

ROGERS 2013
Ed Rogers, *A Short History of Modern Fencing in Scotland*, Edinburgh, 2013; available at www.scottish-fencing.co.uk

RIAS
Royal Incorporation of Architects In Scotland (RIAS) Illustrated Architectural Guides (various authors and dates)

RPS 2007–14
K.M. Brown et al. (eds), *The Records of the Parliaments of Scotland to 1707*, St Andrews, 2007–14; available at www.rps.ac.uk

SHARMAN 2000
Paul Sharman, 'Bowling Green, Chatelherault, South Lanarkshire, watching brief' in *Discovery and Excavation Scotland*, vol.1, Edinburgh, 2000, pp.86–7

SHIELS 1998
Robert S. Shiels, 'The Fatalities at the Ibrox Disaster of 1902' in *The Sports Historian*, vol.18, no.2, Abingdon, November 1998, pp.148–55

SIMPSON 1992
James P. Simpson, *100 Years of Scottish Bowls, 1892–1992*, Aberdeen, 1992

SMITH 1981
David B. Smith, *Curling: An Illustrated History*, Edinburgh, 1981

SMITH 2005
Janet Smith, *Liquid Assets*, London, 2005

SOMERVILLE 1815
James Somerville, *Memorie of the Somervills; being a History of the Baronial House of Somerville* 2 vols, written 1679, published Edinburgh, 1815

SOMERVILLE 1861
Thomas Somerville, *My Own Life and Times, 1741–1814*, written circa 1814, published posthumously, Edinburgh, 1861

STARK 1806
John Stark, *Picture of Edinburgh: Containing a Description of the City and its Environs*, Edinburgh, 1806

STATISTICAL 1791–9
Various authors, First (Old) Statistical Account of Scotland, Edinburgh, 1791–9

STATISTICAL 1834–45
Various authors, Second (New) Statistical Account, Edinburgh, 1834–45

STATISTICAL 1951–92
Various authors, Third Statistical Account of Scotland, Edinburgh, 1951–92

STRATHMORE 1890
Patrick Lyon (ed. A.H. Millar), *The Book of Record – A Diary Written by Patrick First Earl of Strathmore and Other Documents Relating to Glamis Castle 1684–1689*, written 1684–9, published Edinburgh, 1890

THOMSON 1997
Duncan Thomson, *Raeburn*, Edinburgh, 1997

THORBURN 1985
A.M.C. Thorburn, *The Scottish Rugby Union: Official History*, Edinburgh, 1985

TRANTER 1989
Neil L. Tranter, 'The Patronage of Organised Sport in Central Scotland, 1820–1900' in *Journal of Sport History*, vol.16, no.3, Seattle, 1989

VAMPLEW 1982
Wray Vamplew, 'The Economics of a Sports Industry: Scottish Gate-Money Football, 1890–1914' in *The Economic History Review*, new series, vol.35, no.4, London, November 1982, pp.549–67

VAMPLEW 2003
Wray Vamplew, 'Reduced Horse Power: The Jockey Club and the Regulation of British Horseracing' in *Entertainment Law*, vol.2, no.3, Nottingham, 2003, pp.94–111

VAMPLEW 2005
Wray Vamplew et al. (eds), *Encyclopedia of Traditional British Rural Sports*, Abingdon, 2005

WEDDERBURN 1636
David Wedderburn, *Vocabula*, Aberdeen, 1636 (earliest surviving edition Edinburgh, 1685, in the University of Glasgow Library Special Collections)

WEBSTER 1973
David Pirie Webster, *Highland Games – Scotland*, Edinburgh, 1973

WILKES 1819
John Wilkes, *Encyclopaedia Londinensis*, vol.16, London, 1819

Online Resources

GENERAL

Aberdeen City Libraries local studies: www.silvercityvault.org.uk

Am Baile (Highland History & Culture): www.ambaile.org.uk

British Library: www.bl.uk

British Newspaper Archive: www.britishnewspaperarchive.co.uk

Capital Collections (City of Edinburgh): www.capitalcollections.org.uk

Dictionary of Scottish Architects: www.scottisharchitects.org.uk

The Glasgow Story: www.theglasgowstory.com

Historic Scotland: www.historic-scotland.gov.uk

Internet Archive (full text publications): www.archive.org

Jstor* (full text journals): www.jstor.org

Mackintosh Architecture, Context, Making & Meaning: www.mackintosh-architecture.gla.ac.uk

National Galleries of Scotland: www.nationalgalleries.org

National Library of Scotland: www.nls.uk

National Museums of Scotland: www.nms.ac.uk

National Records of Scotland: www.nas.gov.uk

Records of the Parliaments of Scotland to 1707: www.rps.ac.uk

Royal Commission on the Ancient & Historical Monuments of Scotland (RCAHMS): www.rcahms.gov.uk

Scottish Archive Network: www.scan.org.uk

SCRAN (Scottish Cultural Resources Access Network): www.scran.ac.uk

Scotland's Places: www.scotlandsplaces.gov.uk

University of Aberdeen Online Collections: www.digitool.abdn.ac.uk

University of Glasgow Special Collections: www.gla.ac.uk/services/specialcollections

University of St Andrews Special Collections: www.st-andrews.ac.uk/library/specialcollections/

Virtual Mitchell (Mitchell Library, Glasgow): www.mitchelllibrary.org/virtualmitchell

GOVERNING BODIES

A list of Scottish governing bodies can be found on the sportscotland website: www.sportscotland.org.uk

INDIVIDUAL SPORTS

Baths and Washhouses Historical Archive: www.bathsandwashhouses.co.uk

Books on bowls: www.booksonbowls.co.uk

British Golf Museum: www.britishgolfmuseum.co.uk

Historical Curling Places: www.historicalcurlingplaces.org

The Curling Blog (David B. Smith; Bob Cowan): www.curlinghistory.blogspot.co.uk

Golf's Missing Links website: www.golfsmissinglinks.co.uk

Michael Flannery's *Golf – The True History*: www.golftoday.co.uk/history/

Racecourse profiles and closed courses: www.greyhoundderby.com

Scottish Football Museum: www.scottishfootballmuseum.org.uk

Scottish Football Historical Archive: www.scottish-football-historical-archive.com

Scottish Ice Hockey: www.scottishicehockey.net

Victorian Turkish Bath information exchange website: www.victorianturkishbath.org

IMAGE CREDITS

The publisher gratefully acknowledges the following individuals and organisations who have contributed photographic material to this book. Unless stated below, all images reproduced in this book are © Nick Haynes.

Images: page 69 by courtesy of Braemar Gathering Annual; pages 70 and 71 © Ross Brown; pages 88-9 by kind permission of Buro Happold; page 65 by kind permission of Cardross Golf Club; page 14 by permission of East Ayrshire Council; page 19 by permission of Glencoe and North Lorn Folk Museum; pages 21, 39, 40, 62, 68 and 76 © Crown Copyright Historic Scotland; page 23 © Keith Hunter; page 20 by kind permission of the University of Glasgow; pages 34, 60, 80, 100 and 104 by kind permission of the Trustees of the National Galleries of Scotland; page 26 by kind permission of the Trustees of the National Gallery, London; pages 8, 11 and 12 by kind permission of the Trustees of the National Library of Scotland; pages 27 and 34 © the Trustees of the National Museums of Scotland; page 64 © National Railway Museum/Pictorial Collection/ Science & Society Picture Library; page 10 © National Records of Scotland; page 35 © Tom Parnell; pages 58-9 reproduced by permission of the Royal Burgess Golf Club; and page 74 by courtesy of Royal Burgh of Lanark Museum Trust.

The following images from the Royal Commission on the Ancient and Historical Monuments of Scotland (Licensor www.rcahms.gov.uk) have been reproduced: frontispiece (DP 098027) © Crown Copyright; page 6 (SC 358426) © courtesy of RCAHMS (Artist Tom Curr); page15 (DP 149650) © courtesy of RCAHMS; page 16 (DP 071913) © courtesy of RCAHMS; page 17 (SC 1120480) © courtesy of RCAHMS (Scottish Colorfoto Collection); page 18 (SC 696173) © RCAHMS (Henry Bedford Lemere Collection); page 27 (SC 1124441) © Crown Copyright and (SC 357563) © Crown Copyright; page 31 (DP 144509) © RCAHMS (Aerial Photography Collection); page 38 (SC 466242) © Crown Copyright; page 48 (SC 1117794) © Crown Copyright; page 54 (DP 009535) © RCAHMS (Aerial Photography Collection); page 55 (DP 043966) © RCAHMS (Aerial Photography Collection); page 56 (SC 609905) © RCAHMS (Shearer and Annand Collection); page 62 (DP 062736) © Crown Copyright and (DP 151741) © Crown Copyright; page 63 (DP 148 556) © Crown Copyright; pages 72-3 (SC 1206481) © Crown Copyright; page 79 (DP 043403) © RCAHMS (J. and J.A. Carrick Collection); page 81 (DP 104567) © Crown Copyright; page 82 (SC 1115425) © Crown Copyright; page 86 (DP 048136) © RCAHMS (Aerofilms Collection); page 87 (DP 041805) © RCAHMS (Aerial Photography Collection); pages 90-1 (DP 037109) © Crown Copyright; page 92 (SC 681729) © RCAHMS (Henry Bedford Lemere Collection); page 92 (SC 683137) © RCAHMS (Henry Bedford Lemere Collection) and page 93 (DP 004616) © RCAHMS (Alexander Buchanan Campbell Collection).